R Graphics Essentials for Great Data Visualization

Alboukadel KASSAMBARA

ii

Contents

Preface

0.1 What you will learn

Data visualization is one of the most important part of data science. Many books and courses present a catalogue of graphics but they don't teach you which charts to use according to the type of the data.

In this book, we start by presenting the key graphic systems and packages available in R, including R base graphs, lattice and ggplot2 plotting systems.

Next, we provide practical examples to create great graphics for the right data using either the ggplot2 package and extensions or the traditional R graphics.

With this book, you 'll learn:

- How to quickly create beautiful graphics using ggplot2 packages
- How to properly customize and annotate the plots
- Type of graphics for visualizing categorical and continuous variables
- How to add automatically p-values to box plots, bar plots and alternatives
- How to add marginal density plots and correlation coefficients to scatter plots
- Key methods for analyzing and visualizing multivariate data
- R functions and packages for plotting time series data
- How to combine multiple plots on one page to create production-quality figures.

0.2 Book website

The website for this book is located at : `http://www.sthda.com/english/`. It contains number of resources.

0.3 Executing the R codes from the PDF

For a single line R code, you can just copy the code from the PDF to the R console.

For a multiple-line R codes, an error is generated, sometimes, when you copy and paste directly the R code from the PDF to the R console. If this happens, a solution is to:

- Paste firstly the code in your R code editor or in your text editor
- Copy the code from your text/code editor to the R console

0.4 Colophon

This book was built with R 3.3.2 and the following packages :

```
##                 name       version                    source
## 1           bookdown           0.5      Github:rstudio/bookdown
## 2        changepoint         2.2.2                       CRAN
## 3            cowplot   0.8.0.9000      Github:wilkelab/cowplot
## 4              dplyr         0.7.4                       cran
## 5         factoextra   1.0.5.999  local:kassambara/factoextra
## 6          FactoMineR          1.38                       CRAN
## 7             GGally         1.3.0                       CRAN
## 8         ggcorrplot   0.1.1.9000 Github:kassambara/ggcorrplot
## 9            ggforce         0.1.1    Github:thomasp85/ggforce
## 10         ggformula           0.6                       CRAN
## 11         ggfortify         0.4.1                       CRAN
## 12           ggpmisc        0.2.15                       CRAN
## 13            ggpubr     0.1.5.999    Github:kassambara/ggpubr
## 14           lattice       0.20-34                       CRAN
## 15             readr         1.1.1                       cran
## 16      scatterplot3d        0.3-40                       cran
## 17        strucchange         1.5-1                       CRAN
## 18             tidyr         0.7.2                       cran
```

About the author

Alboukadel Kassambara is a PhD in Bioinformatics and Cancer Biology. He works since many years on genomic data analysis and visualization (read more: `http://www.alboukadel.com/`).

He has work experiences in statistical and computational methods to identify prognostic and predictive biomarker signatures through integrative analysis of large-scale genomic and clinical data sets.

He created a bioinformatics web-tool named GenomicScape (www.genomicscape.com) which is an easy-to-use web tool for gene expression data analysis and visualization.

He developed also a training website on data science, named STHDA (Statistical Tools for High-throughput Data Analysis, www.sthda.com/english), which contains many tutorials on data analysis and visualization using R software and packages.

He is the author of many popular R packages for:

- multivariate data analysis (**factoextra**, `http://www.sthda.com/english/rpkgs/factoextra`),
- survival analysis (**survminer**, `http://www.sthda.com/english/rpkgs/survminer/`),
- correlation analysis (**ggcorrplot**, `http://www.sthda.com/english/wiki/ggcorrplot-visualization-of-a-correlation-matrix-using-ggplot2`),
- creating publication ready plots in R (**ggpubr**, `http://www.sthda.com/english/rpkgs/ggpubr`).

Recently, he published three books on data analysis and visualization:

1. Practical Guide to Cluster Analysis in R (`https://goo.gl/yhhpXh`)
2. Practical Guide To Principal Component Methods in R (`https://goo.gl/d4Doz9`)

Chapter 1

R Basics for Data Visualization

1.1 Introduction

R is a free and powerful statistical software for analyzing and visualizing data.

In this chapter, you'll learn:

- the basics of R programming for importing and manipulating your data:
    - filtering and ordering rows,
    - renaming and adding columns,
    - computing summary statistics
- R graphics systems and packages for data visualization:
    - R traditional base plots
    - Lattice plotting system that aims to improve on R base graphics
    - ggplot2 package, a powerful and a flexible R package, for producing elegant graphics piece by piece.
    - ggpubr package, which facilitates the creation of beautiful ggplot2-based graphs for researcher with non-advanced programming backgrounds.
    - ggformula package, an extension of ggplot2, based on formula interfaces (much like the lattice interface)

1.2 Install R and RStudio

RStudio is an integrated development environment for R that makes using R easier. R and RStudio can be installed on Windows, MAC OSX and Linux platforms.

1. R can be downloaded and installed from the Comprehensive R Archive Network (CRAN) webpage (`http://cran.r-project.org/`)
2. After installing R software, install also the RStudio software available at: `http://www.rstudio.com/products/RStudio/`.
3. Launch RStudio and start use R inside R studio.

1.3   Install and load required R packages

An R package is a collection of functionalities that extends the capabilities of base R. To use the R code provide in this book, you should install the following R packages:

- `tidyverse` packages, which are a collection of R packages that share the same programming philosophy. These packages include:
    - `readr`: for importing data into R
    - `dplyr`: for data manipulation
    - `ggplot2` and `ggpubr` for data visualization.
- `ggpubr` package, which makes it easy, for beginner, to create publication ready plots.

1. **Install the tidyverse package**. Installing tidyverse will install automatically readr, dplyr, ggplot2 and more. Type the following code in the R console:

```
install.packages("tidyverse")
```

2. **Install the ggpubr package**.

- We recommend to install the latest developmental version of ggpubr as follow:

```
if(!require(devtools)) install.packages("devtools")
devtools::install_github("kassambara/ggpubr")
```

- If the above R code fails, you can install the latest stable version on CRAN:

```
install.packages("ggpubr")
```

3. **Load required packages**. After installation, you must first load the package for using the functions in the package. The function `library()` is used for this task. An alternative function is `require()`. For example, to load ggplot2 and ggpubr packages, type this:

```
library("ggplot2")
library("ggpubr")
```

Now, we can use R functions, such as *ggscatter()* [in the ggpubr package] for creating a scatter plot.

If you want to learn more about a given function, say ggscatter(), type this in R console: `?ggscatter`.

1.4   Data format

Your data should be in rectangular format, where columns are variables and rows are observations (individuals or samples).

- Column names should be compatible with R naming conventions. Avoid column with blank space and special characters. Good column names: `long_jump` or `long.jump`. Bad column name: `long jump`.

- Avoid beginning column names with a number. Use letter instead. Good column names: `sport_100m` or `x100m`. Bad column name: `100m`.

- Replace missing values by `NA` (for not available)

For example, your data should look like this:

```
  manufacturer model displ year cyl     trans drv
1         audi    a4   1.8 1999   4   auto(l5)   f
2         audi    a4   1.8 1999   4 manual(m5)   f
3         audi    a4   2.0 2008   4 manual(m6)   f
4         audi    a4   2.0 2008   4   auto(av)   f
```

Read more at: Best Practices in Preparing Data Files for Importing into R[1]

1.5 Import your data in R

First, save your data into txt or csv file formats and import it as follow (you will be asked to choose the file):

```
library("readr")

# Reads tab delimited files (.txt tab)
my_data <- read_tsv(file.choose())

# Reads comma (,) delimited files (.csv)
my_data <- read_csv(file.choose())

# Reads semicolon(;) separated files(.csv)
my_data <- read_csv2(file.choose())
```

Read more about how to import data into R at this link: http://www.sthda.com/english/wiki/importing-data-into-r

1.6 Demo data sets

R comes with several demo data sets for playing with R functions. The most used R demo data sets include: **USArrests**, **iris** and **mtcars**. To load a demo data set, use the function **data()** as follow. The function **head()** is used to inspect the data.

```
data("iris")   # Loading
head(iris, n = 3)  # Print the first n = 3 rows
```

```
##   Sepal.Length Sepal.Width Petal.Length Petal.Width Species
## 1          5.1         3.5          1.4         0.2  setosa
## 2          4.9         3.0          1.4         0.2  setosa
```

---

[1]http://www.sthda.com/english/wiki/best-practices-in-preparing-data-files-for-importing-into-r

```
## 3          4.7          3.2          1.3          0.2  setosa
```

To learn more about iris data sets, type this:

```
?iris
```

After typing the above R code, you will see the description of `iris` data set: this iris data set gives the measurements in centimeters of the variables sepal length and width and petal length and width, respectively, for 50 flowers from each of 3 species of iris. The species are Iris setosa, versicolor, and virginica.

1.7   Data manipulation

After importing your data in R, you can easily manipulate it using the `dplyr` package (Wickham et al., 2017), which can be installed using the R code: `install.packages("dplyr")`.

After loading dplyr, you can use the following R functions:

- `filter()`: Pick rows (observations/samples) based on their values.
- `distinct()`: Remove duplicate rows.
- `arrange()`: Reorder the rows.
- `select()`: Select columns (variables) by their names.
- `rename()`: Rename columns.
- `mutate()`: Add/create new variables.
- `summarise()`: Compute statistical summaries (e.g., computing the mean or the sum)
- `group_by()`: Operate on subsets of the data set.

> Note that, dplyr package allows to use the forward-pipe chaining operator (%>%) for combining multiple operations. For example, x %>% f is equivalent to f(x). Using the pipe (%>%), the output of each operation is passed to the next operation. This makes R programming easy.

We'll show you how these functions work in the different chapters of this book.

1.8   R graphics systems

There are different graphic packages available in R[2] for visualizing your data: 1) R base graphs, 2) Lattice Graphs (Sarkar, 2016) and 3) ggplot2 (Wickham and Chang, 2017).

In this section, we start by providing a quick overview of R base and lattice plots, and then we move to ggplot2 graphic system. The vast majority of plots generated in this book is based on the modern and flexible **ggplot2** R package.

---

[2]http://www.sthda.com/english/wiki/data-visualization

1.8.1 R base graphs

R comes with simple functions to create many types of graphs. For example:

Plot Types	R base function
Scatter plot	plot()
Scatter plot matrix	pairs()
Box plot	boxplot()
Strip chart	stripchart()
Histogram plot	hist()
density plot	density()
Bar plot	barplot()
Line plot	plot() and line()
Pie charts	pie()
Dot charts	dotchart()
Add text to a plot	text()

In the most cases, you can use the following arguments to customize the plot:

- `pch`: change point shapes. Allowed values comprise number from 1 to 25.
- `cex`: change point size. Example: `cex = 0.8`.
- `col`: change point color. Example: col = "blue".
- `frame`: logical value. `frame = FALSE` removes the plot panel border frame.
- `main, xlab, ylab`. Specify the main title and the x/y axis labels -, respectively
- `las`: For a vertical x axis text, use `las = 2`.

In the following R code, we'll use the iris data set to create a:

- (1) Scatter plot of Sepal.Length (on x-axis) and Sepal.Width (on y-axis).

- (2) Box plot of Sepal.length (y-axis) by Species (x-axis)

```
# (1) Create a scatter lot
plot(
  x = iris$Sepal.Length, y = iris$Sepal.Width,
  pch = 19, cex = 0.8, frame = FALSE,
  xlab = "Sepal Length",ylab = "Sepal Width"
  )


# (2) Create a box plot
boxplot(Sepal.Length ~ Species, data = iris,
        ylab = "Sepal.Length",
        frame = FALSE, col = "lightgray")
```

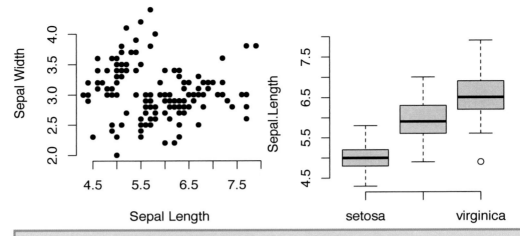

Read more examples at: R base Graphics on STHDA, `http://www.sthda.com/english/wiki/r-base-graphs`

1.8.2   Lattice graphics

The **lattice** R package provides a plotting system that aims to improve on R base graphs. After installing the package, whith the R command `install.packages("lattice")`, you can test the following functions.

- Main functions in the lattice package:

Plot types	Lattice functions
Scatter plot	xyplot()
Scatter plot matrix	splom()
3D scatter plot	cloud()
Box plot	bwplot()
strip plots (1-D scatter plots)	stripplot()
Dot plot	dotplot()
Bar chart	barchart()
Histogram	histogram()
Density plot	densityplot()
Theoretical quantile plot	qqmath()
Two-sample quantile plot	qq()
3D contour plot of surfaces	contourplot()
False color level plot of surfaces	levelplot()
Parallel coordinates plot	parallel()
3D wireframe graph	wireframe()

The lattice package uses formula interface. For example, in lattice terminology, the formula y ~ x | group, means that we want to plot the y variable according to the x variable, splitting the plot into multiple panels by the variable group.

- **Create a basic scatter plot of y by x.** Syntax: `y ~ x`. Change the color by groups and use `auto.key = TRUE` to show legends:

```
library("lattice")
xyplot(
  Sepal.Length ~ Petal.Length, group = Species,
  data = iris, auto.key = TRUE, pch = 19, cex = 0.5
  )
```

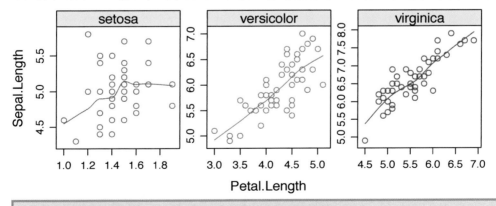

- **Multiple panel plots by groups.** Syntax: `y ~ x | group`.

```
xyplot(
  Sepal.Length ~ Petal.Length | Species,
  layout = c(3, 1),                    # panel with ncol = 3 and nrow = 1
  group = Species, data = iris,
  type = c("p", "smooth"),             # Show points and smoothed line
  scales = "free"                      # Make panels axis scales independent
  )
```

Read more examples at: Lattice Graphics on STHDA[a]

―――――――――
[a]http://www.sthda.com/english/wiki/lattice-graphs

1.8.3   ggplot2 graphics

GGPlot2 is a powerful and a flexible R package, implemented by Hadley Wickham, for producing elegant graphics piece by piece. The **gg** in ggplot2 means *Grammar of Graphics*, a graphic concept which describes plots by using a "grammar". According to the ggplot2 concept, a plot can be divided into different fundamental parts: **Plot = data + Aesthetics + Geometry**

- **data**: a data frame
- **aesthetics**: used to indicate the **x** and **y** variables. It can be also used to control the **color**, the **size** and the **shape** of points, etc.....
- **geometry**: corresponds to the type of graphics (histogram, box plot, line plot, ...)

> The ggplot2 syntax might seem opaque for beginners, but once you understand the basics, you can create and customize any kind of plots you want.
>
> Note that, to reduce this opacity, we recently created an R package, named **ggpubr** (ggplot2 Based Publication Ready Plots), for making ggplot simpler for students and researchers with non-advanced programming backgrounds. We'll present ggpubr in the next section.

After installing and loading the ggplot2 package, you can use the following key functions:

Plot types	GGPlot2 functions
Initialize a ggplot	ggplot()
Scatter plot	geom_point()
Box plot	geom_boxplot()
Violin plot	geom_violin()
strip chart	geom_jitter()
Dot plot	geom_dotplot()
Bar chart	geom_bar()
Line plot	geom_line()
Histogram	geom_histogram()
Density plot	geom_density()
Error bars	geom_errorbar()
QQ plot	stat_qq()
ECDF plot	stat_ecdf()
Title and axis labels	labs()

The main function in the ggplot2 package is `ggplot()`, which can be used to initialize the plotting system with data and x/y variables.

For example, the following R code takes the `iris` data set to initialize the ggplot and then a layer (`geom_point()`) is added onto the ggplot to create a scatter plot of x = Sepal.Length by y = Sepal.Width:

```
library(ggplot2)
ggplot(iris, aes(x = Sepal.Length, y = Sepal.Width))+
  geom_point()
```

```
# Change point size, color and shape
ggplot(iris, aes(x = Sepal.Length, y = Sepal.Width))+
  geom_point(size = 1.2, color = "steelblue", shape = 21)
```

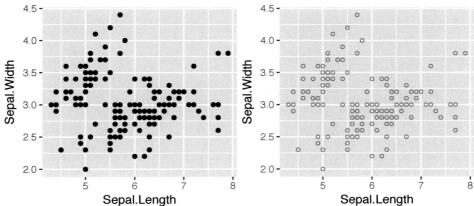

Note that, in the code above, the shape of points is specified as number. To display the different point shape available in R, type this:

```
ggpubr::show_point_shapes()
```

It's also possible to control points shape and color by a grouping variable (here, Species). For example, in the code below, we map points color and shape to the Species grouping variable.

```
# Control points color by groups
ggplot(iris, aes(x = Sepal.Length, y = Sepal.Width))+
  geom_point(aes(color = Species, shape = Species))
```

```
# Change the default color manually.
# Use the scale_color_manual() function
ggplot(iris, aes(x = Sepal.Length, y = Sepal.Width))+
  geom_point(aes(color = Species, shape = Species))+
  scale_color_manual(values = c("#00AFBB", "#E7B800", "#FC4E07"))
```

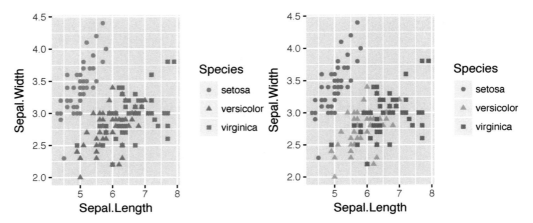

You can also split the plot into multiple panels according to a grouping variable. R function: `facet_wrap()`. Another interesting feature of ggplot2, is the possibility to combine multiple layers on the same plot. For example, with the following R code, we'll:

- Add points with `geom_point()`, colored by groups.
- Add the fitted smoothed regression line using `geom_smooth()`. By default the function `geom_smooth()` add the regression line and the confidence area. You can control the line color and confidence area fill color by groups.
- Facet the plot into multiple panels by groups
- Change color and fill manually using the function `scale_color_manual()` and `scale_fill_manual()`

```
ggplot(iris, aes(x = Sepal.Length, y = Sepal.Width))+
  geom_point(aes(color = Species))+
  geom_smooth(aes(color = Species, fill = Species))+
  facet_wrap(~Species, ncol = 3, nrow = 1)+
  scale_color_manual(values = c("#00AFBB", "#E7B800", "#FC4E07"))+
  scale_fill_manual(values = c("#00AFBB", "#E7B800", "#FC4E07"))
```

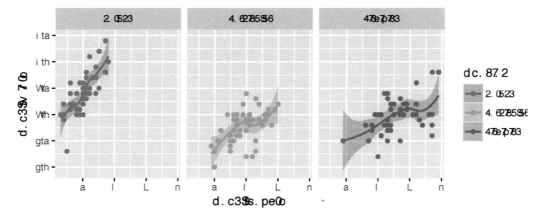

Note that, the default theme of ggplots is `theme_gray()` (or `theme_grey()`), which is theme with grey background and white grid lines. More themes are available for professional presentations or publications. These include: `theme_bw()`, `theme_classic()` and

```
theme_minimal().
```

To change the theme of a given ggplot (p), use this: `p + theme_classic()`. To change the default theme to `theme_classic()` for all the future ggplots during your entire R session, type the following R code:

```
theme_set(
  theme_classic()
)
```

Now you can create ggplots with `theme_classic()` as default theme:

```
ggplot(iris, aes(x = Sepal.Length, y = Sepal.Width))+
  geom_point()
```

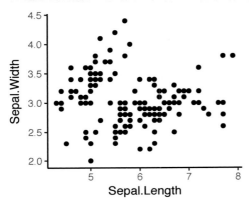

1.8.4 ggpubr for publication ready plots

The **ggpubr** R package facilitates the creation of beautiful ggplot2-based graphs for researcher with non-advanced programming backgrounds (Kassambara, 2017).

For example, to create the density distribution of "Sepal.Length", colored by groups ("Species"), type this:

```
library(ggpubr)
# Density plot with mean lines and marginal rug
ggdensity(iris, x = "Sepal.Length",
    add = "mean", rug = TRUE,            # Add mean line and marginal rugs
    color = "Species", fill = "Species", # Color by groups
    palette = "jco")                     # use jco journal color palette
```

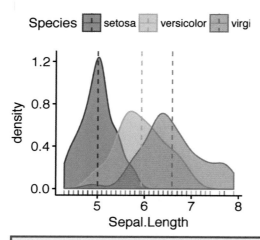

Note that the argument `palette` can take also a custom color palette. For example `palette= c("#00AFBB", "#E7B800", "#FC4E07")`.

- Create a box plot with p-values comparing groups:

```
# Groups that we want to compare
my_comparisons <- list(
  c("setosa", "versicolor"), c("versicolor", "virginica"),
  c("setosa", "virginica")
)

# Create the box plot. Change colors by groups: Species
# Add jitter points and change the shape by groups
ggboxplot(
  iris, x = "Species", y = "Sepal.Length",
  color = "Species", palette = c("#00AFBB", "#E7B800", "#FC4E07"),
  add = "jitter"
  )+
  stat_compare_means(comparisons = my_comparisons, method = "t.test")
```

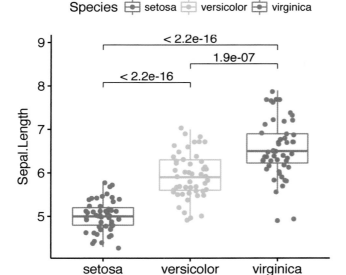

Learn more on STHDA at: ggpubr: Publication Ready Plots[a]

[a]http://www.sthda.com/english/articles/24-ggpubr-publication-ready-plots/

1.9 Export R graphics

You can export R graphics to many file formats, including: PDF, PostScript, SVG vector files, Windows MetaFile (WMF), PNG, TIFF, JPEG, etc.

The standard procedure to save any graphics from R is as follow:

1. **Open a graphic device** using one of the following functions:

- pdf("r-graphics.pdf"),
- postscript("r-graphics.ps"),
- svg("r-graphics.svg"),
- png("r-graphics.png"),
- tiff("r-graphics.tiff"),
- jpeg("r-graphics.jpg"),
- win.metafile("r-graphics.wmf"),
- and so on.

Additional arguments indicating the width and the height (in inches) of the graphics region can be also specified in the mentioned function.

2. **Create a plot**

3. **Close the graphic device** using the function `dev.off()`

For example, you can export R base plots to a pdf file as follow:

```
pdf("r-base-plot.pdf")
# Plot 1 --> in the first page of PDF
plot(x = iris$Sepal.Length, y = iris$Sepal.Width)
# Plot 2 ---> in the second page of the PDF
hist(iris$Sepal.Length)
dev.off()
```

To export ggplot2 graphs, the R code looks like this:

```
# Create some plots
library(ggplot2)
myplot1 <- ggplot(iris, aes(Sepal.Length, Sepal.Width)) +
  geom_point()
myplot2 <- ggplot(iris, aes(Species, Sepal.Length)) +
  geom_boxplot()

# Print plots to a pdf file
pdf("ggplot.pdf")
print(myplot1)      # Plot 1 --> in the first page of PDF
print(myplot2)      # Plot 2 ---> in the second page of the PDF
dev.off()
```

Note that for a ggplot, you can also use the following functions to export the graphic:

- ggsave() [in ggplot2]. Makes it easy to save a ggplot. It guesses the type of graphics device from the file extension.
- ggexport() [in ggpubr]. Makes it easy to arrange and export multiple ggplots at once.

> See also the following blog post to save high-resolution ggplots[a]
>
> ---
>
> [a]http://www.sthda.com/english/wiki/saving-high-resolution-ggplots-how-to-preserve-semi-transparency

Chapter 2

Plot One Variable

2.1 Introduction

To visualize one variable, the type of graphs to be used depends on the type of the variable:

- For **categorical variable** or grouping variables. You can visualize the count of categories using a bar plot or using a pie chart to show the proportion of each category.
- For **continuous variable**, you can visualize the distribution of the variable using density plots, histograms and alternatives.

In this R graphics tutorial, you'll learn how to:

- Visualize a categorical variable using bar plots, dot charts and pie charts
- Visualize the distribution of a continuous variable using:
  - density and histogram plots,
  - other alternatives, such as frequency polygon, area plots, dot plots, box plots, Empirical cumulative distribution function (ECDF) and Quantile-quantile plot (QQ plots).
  - Density ridgeline plots, which are useful for visualizing changes in distributions, of a continuous variable, over time or space.
  - Bar plot and modern alternatives, including lollipop charts and cleveland's dot plots.

2.2 Prerequisites

Load required packages and set the theme function `theme_pubr()` [in ggpubr] as the default theme:

```
library(ggplot2)
library(ggpubr)
theme_set(theme_pubr())
```

2.3   One categorical variable

2.3.1   Bar plot of counts

- Plot types: Bar plot of the count of group levels
- Key function: `geom_bar()`
- Key arguments: `alpha`, `color`, `fill`, `linetype` and `size`

Demo data set: `diamonds` [in ggplot2]. Contains the prices and other attributes of almost 54000 diamonds. The column `cut` contains the quality of the diamonds cut (Fair, Good, Very Good, Premium, Ideal).

The R code below creates a bar plot visualizing the number of elements in each category of diamonds cut.

```
ggplot(diamonds, aes(cut)) +
  geom_bar(fill = "#0073C2FF") +
  theme_pubclean()
```

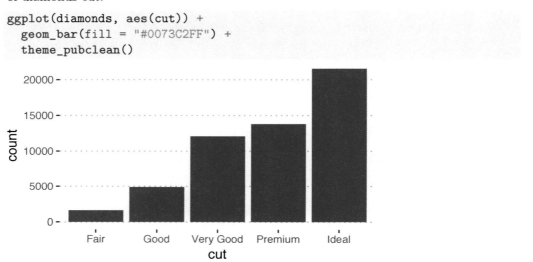

Compute the frequency of each category and add the labels on the bar plot:

- `dplyr` package used to summarise the data
- `geom_bar()` with option `stat = "identity"` is used to create the bar plot of the summary output as it is.
- `geom_text()` used to add text labels. Adjust the position of the labels by using `hjust` (horizontal justification) and `vjust` (vertical justification). Values should be in [0, 1].

```
# Compute the frequency
library(dplyr)
df <- diamonds %>%
  group_by(cut) %>%
  summarise(counts = n())
df
```

```
## # A tibble: 5 x 2
##        cut counts
##      <ord>  <int>
```

```
## 1      Fair    1610
## 2      Good    4906
## 3 Very Good   12082
## 4   Premium   13791
## 5     Ideal   21551
```

```
# Create the bar plot. Use theme_pubclean() [in ggpubr]
ggplot(df, aes(x = cut, y = counts)) +
  geom_bar(fill = "#0073C2FF", stat = "identity") +
  geom_text(aes(label = counts), vjust = -0.3) +
  theme_pubclean()
```

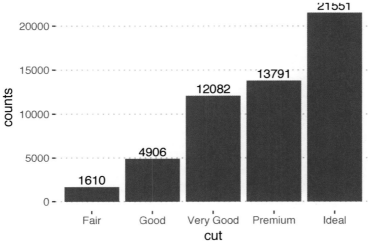

2.3.2 Pie charts

Pie chart is just a stacked bar chart in polar coordinates.

First,

- Arrange the grouping variable (`cut`) in descending order. This important to compute the y coordinates of labels.
- compute the proportion (counts/total) of each category
- compute the position of the text labels as the cumulative sum of the proportion. To put the labels in the center of pies, we'll use `cumsum(prop) - 0.5*prop` as label position.

```
df <- df %>%
  arrange(desc(cut)) %>%
  mutate(prop = round(counts*100/sum(counts), 1),
         lab.ypos = cumsum(prop) - 0.5*prop)
head(df, 4)
```

```
## # A tibble: 4 x 4
##        cut counts  prop lab.ypos
```

```
##          <ord>  <int>  <dbl>    <dbl>
## 1        Ideal  21551  40.0     20.0
## 2      Premium  13791  25.6     52.8
## 3    Very Good  12082  22.4     76.8
## 4         Good   4906   9.1     92.5
```

- Create the pie charts using ggplot2 verbs. Key function: `coord_polar()`.

```
ggplot(df, aes(x = "", y = prop, fill = cut)) +
  geom_bar(width = 1, stat = "identity", color = "white") +
  geom_text(aes(y = lab.ypos, label = prop), color = "white")+
  coord_polar("y", start = 0)+
  ggpubr::fill_palette("jco")+
  theme_void()
```

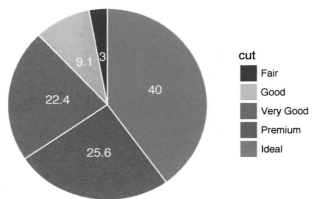

- Alternative solution to easily create a pie chart: use the function **ggpie()** [in gg-pubr]:

```
ggpie(
  df, x = "prop", label = "prop",
  lab.pos = "in", lab.font = list(color = "white"),
  fill = "cut", color = "white",
  palette = "jco"
)
```

2.3.3 Dot charts

Dot chart is an alternative to bar plots. Key functions:

- `geom_linerange()`:Creates line segments from x to ymax
- `geom_point()`: adds dots
- `ggpubr::color_palette()`: changes color palette.

```
ggplot(df, aes(cut, prop)) +
  geom_linerange(
    aes(x = cut, ymin = 0, ymax = prop),
    color = "lightgray", size = 1.5
```

```
  )+
geom_point(aes(color = cut), size = 2)+
ggpubr::color_palette("jco")+
theme_pubclean()
```

Easy alternative to create a dot chart. Use **ggdotchart()** [ggpubr]:

```
ggdotchart(
  df, x = "cut", y = "prop",
  color = "cut", size = 3,          # Points color and size
  add = "segment",                  # Add line segments
  add.params = list(size = 2),
  palette = "jco",
  ggtheme = theme_pubclean()
)
```

2.4   One continuous variable

Different types of graphs can be used to visualize the distribution of a continuous variable, including: density and histogram plots.

2.4.1   Data format

Create some data (**wdata**) containing the weights by sex (M for male; F for female):

```
set.seed(1234)
wdata = data.frame(
        sex = factor(rep(c("F", "M"), each=200)),
        weight = c(rnorm(200, 55), rnorm(200, 58))
        )

head(wdata, 4)
```

```
##    sex weight
## 1   F   53.8
## 2   F   55.3
## 3   F   56.1
## 4   F   52.7
```

Compute the mean weight by sex using the `dplyr` package. First, the data is grouped by sex and then summarized by computing the mean weight by groups. The operator `%>%` is used to combine multiple operations:

```
library("dplyr")
mu <- wdata %>%
  group_by(sex) %>%
  summarise(grp.mean = mean(weight))
mu
```

```
## # A tibble: 2 x 2
##       sex grp.mean
##    <fctr>    <dbl>
## 1       F     54.9
## 2       M     58.1
```

2.4.2 Basic plots

We start by creating a plot, named `a`, that we'll finish in the next section by adding a layer.

```
a <- ggplot(wdata, aes(x = weight))
```

Possible layers include: `geom_density()` (for density plots) and `geom_histogram()` (for histogram plots).

Key arguments to customize the plots:

- `color, size, linetype`: change the line color, size and type, respectively
- `fill`: change the areas fill color (for bar plots, histograms and density plots)
- `alpha`: create a semi-transparent color.

2.4.3 Density plots

Key function: `geom_density()`.

1. **Create basic density plots**. Add a vertical line corresponding to the mean value of the weight variable (`geom_vline()`):

```
# y axis scale = ..density.. (default behaviour)
a + geom_density() +
  geom_vline(aes(xintercept = mean(weight)),
             linetype = "dashed", size = 0.6)
```

```
# Change y axis to count instead of density
a + geom_density(aes(y = ..count..), fill = "lightgray") +
  geom_vline(aes(xintercept = mean(weight)),
             linetype = "dashed", size = 0.6,
             color = "#FC4E07")
```

2. **Change areas fill and add line color by groups** (sex):

- Add vertical mean lines using `geom_vline()`. Data: `mu`, which contains the mean values of weights by sex (computed in the previous section).
- Change color manually:
  - use `scale_color_manual()` or `scale_colour_manual()` for changing line color
  - use `scale_fill_manual()` for changing area fill colors.

```
# Change line color by sex
a + geom_density(aes(color = sex)) +
  scale_color_manual(values = c("#868686FF", "#EFC000FF"))
```

```
# Change fill color by sex and add mean line
# Use semi-transparent fill: alpha = 0.4
a + geom_density(aes(fill = sex), alpha = 0.4) +
      geom_vline(aes(xintercept = grp.mean, color = sex),
             data = mu, linetype = "dashed") +
  scale_color_manual(values = c("#868686FF", "#EFC000FF"))+
  scale_fill_manual(values = c("#868686FF", "#EFC000FF"))
```

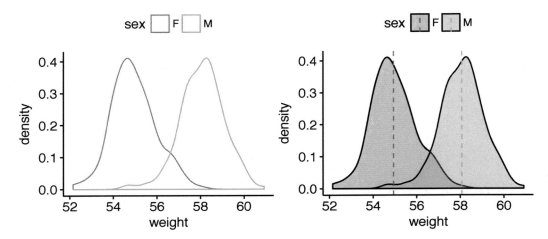

3. **Simple solution to create a ggplot2-based density plots**: use `ggboxplot()`
   [in ggpubr].

```
library(ggpubr)

# Basic density plot with mean line and marginal rug
ggdensity(wdata, x = "weight",
          fill = "#0073C2FF", color = "#0073C2FF",
          add = "mean", rug = TRUE)

# Change outline and fill colors by groups ("sex")
# Use a custom palette
ggdensity(wdata, x = "weight",
   add = "mean", rug = TRUE,
   color = "sex", fill = "sex",
   palette = c("#0073C2FF", "#FC4E07"))
```

2.4.4 Histogram plots

An alternative to density plots is histograms, which represents the distribution of a continuous variable by dividing into bins and counting the number of observations in each bin.

Key function: `geom_histogram()`. The basic usage is quite similar to `geom_density()`.

1. **Create a basic plots.** Add a vertical line corresponding to the mean value of the weight variable:

```
a + geom_histogram(bins = 30, color = "black", fill = "gray") +
  geom_vline(aes(xintercept = mean(weight)),
             linetype = "dashed", size = 0.6)
```

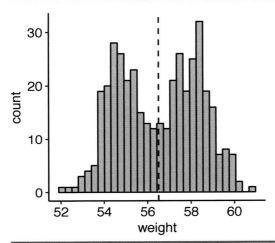

Note that, by default:

- By default, `geom_histogram()` uses 30 bins - this might not be good default. You can change the number of bins (e.g.: bins = 50) or the bin width (e.g.: binwidth = 0.5)
- The y axis corresponds to the count of weight values. If you want to change the plot in order to have the density on y axis, specify the argument `y = ..density..` in `aes()`.

2. **Change areas fill and add line color by groups** (sex):

- Add vertical mean lines using `geom_vline()`. Data: `mu`, which contains the mean values of weights by sex.
- Change color manually:
    - use `scale_color_manual()` or `scale_colour_manual()` for changing line color
    - use `scale_fill_manual()` for changing area fill colors.
- Adjust the position of histogram bars by using the argument `position`. Allowed values: "identity", "stack", "dodge". Default value is "stack".

```
# Change line color by sex
a + geom_histogram(aes(color = sex), fill = "white",
                    position = "identity") +
  scale_color_manual(values = c("#00AFBB", "#E7B800"))

# change fill and outline color manually
a + geom_histogram(aes(color = sex, fill = sex),
                    alpha = 0.4, position = "identity") +
  scale_fill_manual(values = c("#00AFBB", "#E7B800")) +
  scale_color_manual(values = c("#00AFBB", "#E7B800"))
```

3. **Combine histogram and density plots**:

- Plot histogram with density values on y-axis (instead of count values).
- Add density plot with transparent density plot

```
# Histogram with density plot
a + geom_histogram(aes(y = ..density..),
                    colour="black", fill="white") +
  geom_density(alpha = 0.2, fill = "#FF6666")


# Color by groups
a + geom_histogram(aes(y = ..density.., color = sex),
                    fill = "white",
                    position = "identity")+
  geom_density(aes(color = sex), size = 1) +
  scale_color_manual(values = c("#868686FF", "#EFC000FF"))
```

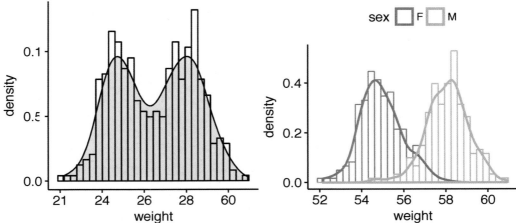

4. **Simple solution to create a ggplot2-based histogram plots**: use gghistogram() [in ggpubr].

```
library(ggpubr)
```

```
# Basic histogram plot with mean line and marginal rug
gghistogram(wdata, x = "weight", bins = 30,
            fill = "#0073C2FF", color = "#0073C2FF",
            add = "mean", rug = TRUE)
```

```
# Change outline and fill colors by groups ("sex")
# Use a custom palette
gghistogram(wdata, x = "weight", bins = 30,
   add = "mean", rug = TRUE,
   color = "sex", fill = "sex",
   palette = c("#0073C2FF", "#FC4E07"))
```

2.4.5 Alternative to density and histogram plots

1. **Frequency polygon**. Very close to histogram plots, but it uses lines instead of bars.
   - Key function: `geom_freqpoly()`.
   - Key arguments: `color`, `size`, `linetype`: change, respectively, line color, size and type.
2. **Area plots**. This is a continuous analog of a stacked bar plot.
   - Key function: `geom_area()`.
   - Key arguments:
     - `color`, `size`, `linetype`: change, respectively, line color, size and type.
     - `fill`: change area fill color.

In this section, we'll use the theme `theme_pubclean()` [in ggpubr]. This is a theme without axis lines, to direct more attention to the data. Type this to use the theme:

```
theme_set(theme_pubclean())
```

- Create a basic frequency polygon and basic area plots:

```
# Basic frequency polygon
a + geom_freqpoly(bins = 30)

# Basic area plots, which can be filled by color
a + geom_area( stat = "bin", bins = 30,
               color = "black", fill = "#00AFBB")
```

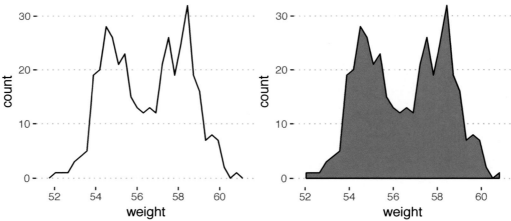

- Change colors by groups (sex):

```
# Frequency polygon:
# Change line colors and types by groups
a + geom_freqpoly( aes(color = sex, linetype = sex),
                   bins = 30, size = 1.5) +
  scale_color_manual(values = c("#00AFBB", "#E7B800"))

# Area plots: change fill colors by sex
```

```
# Create a stacked area plots
a + geom_area(aes(fill = sex), color = "white",
              stat ="bin", bins = 30) +
  scale_fill_manual(values = c("#00AFBB", "#E7B800"))
```

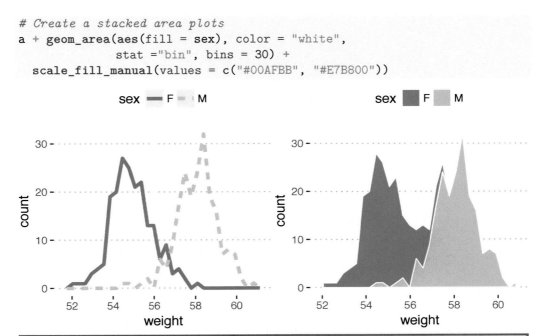

> As in histogram plots, the default y values is count. To have density values on y axis, specify `y = ..density..` in `aes()`.

3. **Dot plots**. Represents another alternative to histograms and density plots, that can be used to visualize a continuous variable. Dots are stacked with each dot representing one observation. The width of a dot corresponds to the bin width.

- Key function: `geom_dotplot()`.
- Key arguments: `alpha`, `color`, `fill` and `dotsize`.

Create a dot plot colored by groups (sex):

```
a + geom_dotplot(aes(fill = sex), binwidth = 1/4) +
  scale_fill_manual(values = c("#00AFBB", "#E7B800"))
```

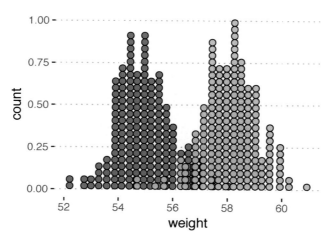

4. **Box plot**:
   - Create a box plot of one continuous variable: `geom_boxplot()`

   - Add jittered points, where each point corresponds to an individual observation:
     `geom_jitter()`. Change the color and the shape of points by groups (sex)

```
ggplot(wdata, aes(x = factor(1), y = weight)) +
  geom_boxplot(width = 0.4, fill = "white") +
  geom_jitter(aes(color = sex, shape = sex),
              width = 0.1, size = 1) +
  scale_color_manual(values = c("#00AFBB", "#E7B800")) +
  labs(x = NULL)    # Remove x axis label
```

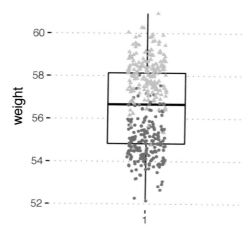

5. **Empirical cumulative distribution function (ECDF)**. Provides another alternative visualization of distribution. It reports for any given number the percent

of individuals that are below that threshold.

For example, in the following plots, you can see that:

- about 25% of our females are shorter than 50 inches
- about 50% of males are shorter than 58 inches

```
# Another option for geom = "point"
a + stat_ecdf(aes(color = sex,linetype = sex),
              geom = "step", size = 1.5) +
  scale_color_manual(values = c("#00AFBB", "#E7B800"))+
  labs(y = "f(weight)")
```

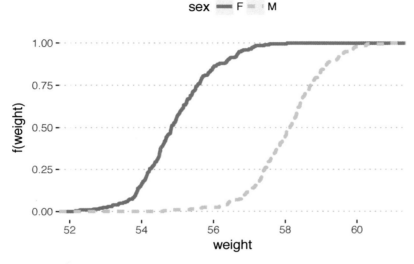

6. **Quantile-quantile plot** (QQ plots). Used to check whether a given data follows normal distribution.

- Key function: `stat_qq()`.
- Key arguments: `color`, `shape` and `size` to change point color, shape and size.

Create a qq-plot of weight. Change color by groups (sex)

```
# Change point shapes by groups
ggplot(wdata, aes(sample = weight)) +
  stat_qq(aes(color = sex)) +
  scale_color_manual(values = c("#00AFBB", "#E7B800"))+
  labs(y = "Weight")
```

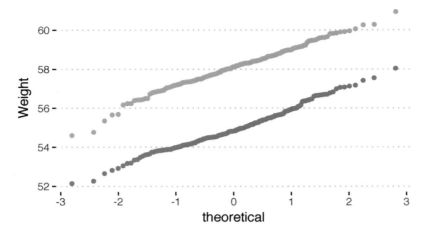

Alternative plot using the function `ggqqplot()` [in ggpubr]. The 95% confidence band is shown by default.

```
library(ggpubr)
ggqqplot(wdata, x = "weight",
    color = "sex",
    palette = c("#0073C2FF", "#FC4E07"),
    ggtheme = theme_pubclean())
```

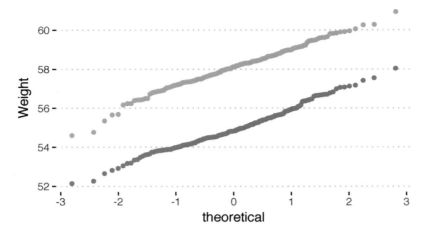

2.4.6   Density ridgeline plots

The density ridgeline plot is an alternative to the standard `geom_density()` function that can be useful for visualizing changes in distributions, of a continuous variable, over time or space. Ridgeline plots are partially overlapping line plots that create the impression of a mountain range.

This functionality is provided in the R package **ggridges** (Wilke, 2017).

1. **Installation**:

```
install.packages("ggridges")
```

2. **Load and set the default theme** to theme_ridges() [in ggridges]:

```
library(ggplot2)
library(ggridges)
theme_set(theme_ridges())
```

3. **Example 1: Simple distribution plots by groups**. Distribution of Sepal.Length by Species using the iris data set. The grouping variable Species will be mapped to the y-axis:

```
ggplot(iris, aes(x = Sepal.Length, y = Species)) +
  geom_density_ridges(aes(fill = Species)) +
  scale_fill_manual(values = c("#00AFBB", "#E7B800", "#FC4E07"))
```

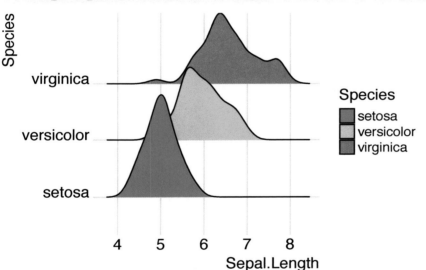

> You can control the overlap between the different densities using the **scale** option. Default value is 1. Smaller values create a separation between the curves, and larger values create more overlap.

```
ggplot(iris, aes(x = Sepal.Length, y = Species)) +
  geom_density_ridges(scale = 0.9)
```

4. **Example 4: Visualize temperature data**.

- Data set: lincoln_weather [in ggridges]. Weather in Lincoln, Nebraska in 2016.

- Create the density ridge plots of the Mean Temperature by Month and change the

fill color according to the temperature value (on x axis). A gradient color is created
using the function `geom_density_ridges_gradient()`

```
ggplot(
  lincoln_weather,
  aes(x = `Mean Temperature [F]`, y = `Month`)
  ) +
geom_density_ridges_gradient(
    aes(fill = ..x..), scale = 3, size = 0.3
    ) +
scale_fill_gradientn(
    colours = c("#0D0887FF", "#CC4678FF", "#F0F921FF"),
    name = "Temp. [F]"
    )+
labs(title = 'Temperatures in Lincoln NE')
```

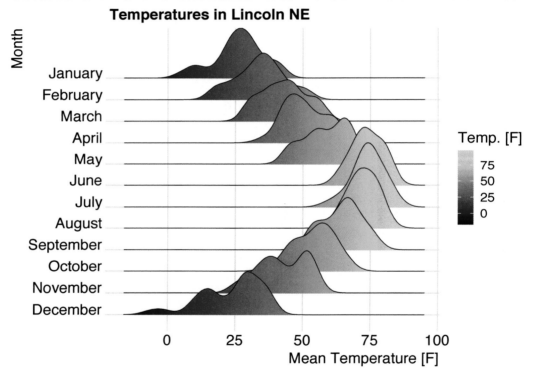

For more examples, type the following R code:

```
browseVignettes("ggridges")
```

2.4.7   Bar plot and modern alternatives

In this section, we'll describe how to create easily basic and ordered bar plots using ggplot2
based helper functions available in the ggpubr R package. We'll also present some modern
alternatives to bar plots, including lollipop charts and cleveland's dot plots.

- Load required packages:

```
library(ggpubr)
```

- Load and prepare data:

```
# Load data
dfm <- mtcars
# Convert the cyl variable to a factor
dfm$cyl <- as.factor(dfm$cyl)
# Add the name colums
dfm$name <- rownames(dfm)
# Inspect the data
head(dfm[, c("name", "wt", "mpg", "cyl")])
```

```
##                               name   wt  mpg cyl
## Mazda RX4                Mazda RX4 2.62 21.0   6
## Mazda RX4 Wag        Mazda RX4 Wag 2.88 21.0   6
## Datsun 710              Datsun 710 2.32 22.8   4
## Hornet 4 Drive      Hornet 4 Drive 3.21 21.4   6
## Hornet Sportabout Hornet Sportabout 3.44 18.7   8
## Valiant                    Valiant 3.46 18.1   6
```

- Create an ordered bar plot of the mpg variable. Change the fill color by the grouping variable "cyl". Sorting will be done globally, but not by groups.

```
ggbarplot(dfm, x = "name", y = "mpg",
          fill = "cyl",                # change fill color by cyl
          color = "white",             # Set bar border colors to white
          palette = "jco",             # jco journal color palett. see ?ggpar
          sort.val = "asc",            # Sort the value in dscending order
          sort.by.groups = TRUE,       # Don't sort inside each group
          x.text.angle = 90,           # Rotate vertically x axis texts
          ggtheme = theme_pubclean()
          )+
  font("x.text", size = 8, vjust = 0.5)
```

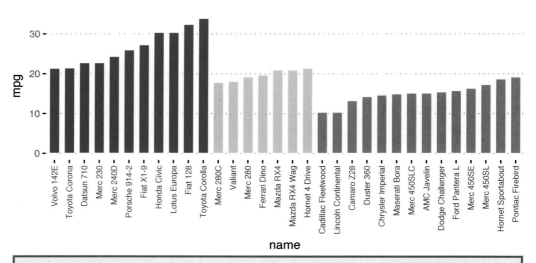

To sort bars inside each group, use the argument **sort.by.groups = TRUE**

- Create a Lollipop chart:
    - Color by groups and set a custom color palette.
    - Sort values in ascending order.
    - Add segments from y = 0 to dots. Change segment color and size.

```
ggdotchart(dfm, x = "name", y = "mpg",
           color = "cyl",
           palette = c("#00AFBB", "#E7B800", "#FC4E07"),
           sorting = "asc", sort.by.groups = TRUE,
           add = "segments",
           add.params = list(color = "lightgray", size = 2),
           group = "cyl",
           dot.size = 4,
           ggtheme = theme_pubclean()
           )+
   font("x.text", size = 8, vjust = 0.5)
```

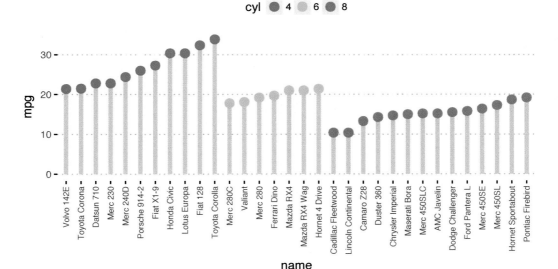

Read more: Bar Plots and Modern Alternatives[1]

2.5 Conclusion

- Create a bar plot of a grouping variable:

```
ggplot(diamonds, aes(cut)) +
  geom_bar(fill = "#0073C2FF") +
  theme_minimal()
```

- Visualize a continuous variable:

Start by creating a plot, named `a`, that we'll be finished by adding a layer.

```
a <- ggplot(wdata, aes(x = weight))
```

Possible layers include:

- **geom_density()**: density plot
- **geom_histogram()**: histogram plot
- **geom_freqpoly()**: frequency polygon
- **geom_area()**: area plot
- **geom_dotplot()**: dot plot
- **stat_ecdf()**: empirical cumulative density function
- **stat_qq()**: quantile - quantile plot

Key arguments to customize the plots:

- `color, size, linetype`: change the line color, size and type, respectively
- `fill`: change the areas fill color (for bar plots, histograms and density plots)

---

[1]`https://goo.gl/eSggcW`

- `alpha`: create a semi-transparent color.

a + geom_density()   **a + geom_histogram()**   **a + geom_freqpoly()**   **a + geom_area()**

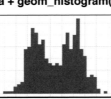   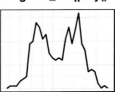      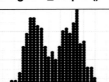

a + geom_dotplot()   **a + stat_ecdf()**   **x + stat_qq()**

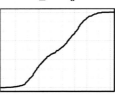   

Chapter 3

Plot Grouped Data

3.1 Introduction

In this chapter, we start by describing how to plot grouped or stacked frequencies of two categorical variables. Tis can be done using bar plots and dot charts. You'll also learn how to add labels to dodged and stacked bar plots.

Next we'll show how to display a continuous variable with multiple groups. In this situation, the grouping variable is used as the x-axis and the continuous variable as the y-axis. You'll learn, how to:

- Visualize a grouped continuous variable using **box plot**, **violin plots**, **stripcharts** and alternatives.
- Add automatically t-test / wilcoxon test p-values comparing groups.
- Create mean and median plots of groups with error bars

3.2 Prerequisites

Load required packages and set the theme function `theme_pubclean()` [in ggpubr] as the default theme:

```
library(dplyr)
library(ggplot2)
library(ggpubr)
theme_set(theme_pubclean())
```

3.3 Grouped categorical variables

- Plot types: grouped bar plots of the frequencies of the categories. Key function: `geom_bar()`.
- Demo dataset: `diamonds` [in ggplot2]. The categorical variables to be used in the demo example are:

– `cut`: quality of the diamonds cut (Fair, Good, Very Good, Premium, Ideal)
– `color`: diamond colour, from J (worst) to D (best).

In our demo example, we'll plot only a subset of the data (color J and D). The different steps are as follow:

- Filter the data to keep only diamonds which colors are in ("J", "D").
- Group the data by the quality of the cut and the diamond color
- Count the number of records by groups
- Create the bar plot

1. **Filter and count the number of records by groups**:

```
df <- diamonds %>%
  filter(color %in% c("J", "D")) %>%
  group_by(cut, color) %>%
  summarise(counts = n())
head(df, 4)
```

```
## # A tibble: 4 x 3
## # Groups:    cut [2]
##      cut color counts
##    <ord> <ord>  <int>
## 1   Fair     D    163
## 2   Fair     J    119
## 3   Good     D    662
## 4   Good     J    307
```

2. **Creare the grouped bar plots**:
   - Key function: `geom_bar()`. Key argument: `stat = "identity"` to plot the data as it is.
   - Use the functions `scale_color_manual()` and `scale_fill_manual()` to set manually the bars border line colors and area fill colors.

```
# Stacked bar plots of y = counts by x = cut,
# colored by the variable color
ggplot(df, aes(x = cut, y = counts)) +
  geom_bar(
    aes(color = color, fill = color),
    stat = "identity", position = position_stack()
    ) +
  scale_color_manual(values = c("#0073C2FF", "#EFC000FF"))+
  scale_fill_manual(values = c("#0073C2FF", "#EFC000FF"))

# Use position = position_dodge()
p <- ggplot(df, aes(x = cut, y = counts)) +
  geom_bar(
    aes(color = color, fill = color),
    stat = "identity", position = position_dodge(0.8),
    width = 0.7
    ) +
```

```
scale_color_manual(values = c("#0073C2FF", "#EFC000FF"))+
scale_fill_manual(values = c("#0073C2FF", "#EFC000FF"))
p
```

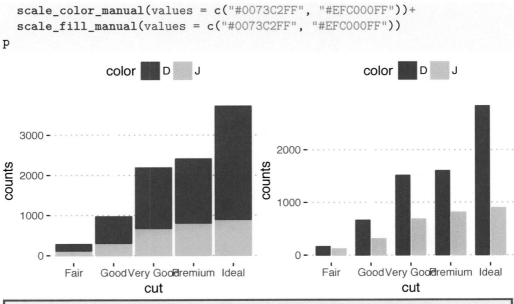

Note that, `position_stack()` automatically stack values in reverse order of the group aesthetic. This default ensures that bar colors align with the default legend. You can change this behavior by using `position = position_stack(reverse = TRUE)`.

Alternatively, you can easily create a dot chart with the **ggpubr** package:

```
ggdotchart(df, x = "cut", y ="counts",
           color = "color", palette = "jco", size = 3,
           add = "segment",
           add.params = list(color = "lightgray", size = 1.5),
           position = position_dodge(0.3),
           ggtheme = theme_pubclean()
           )
```

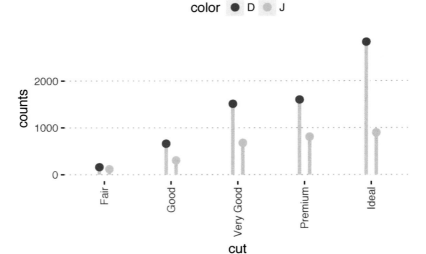

Or, if you prefer the ggplot2 verbs, type this:

```
ggplot(df, aes(cut, counts)) +
  geom_linerange(
    aes(x = cut, ymin = 0, ymax = counts, group = color),
    color = "lightgray", size = 1.5,
    position = position_dodge(0.3)
    )+
  geom_point(
    aes(color = color),
    position = position_dodge(0.3), size = 3
    )+
  scale_color_manual(values = c("#0073C2FF", "#EFC000FF"))+
  theme_pubclean()
```

3. **Add labels to the dodged bar plots**:

```
p + geom_text(
  aes(label = counts, group = color),
  position = position_dodge(0.8),
  vjust = -0.3, size = 3.5
)
```

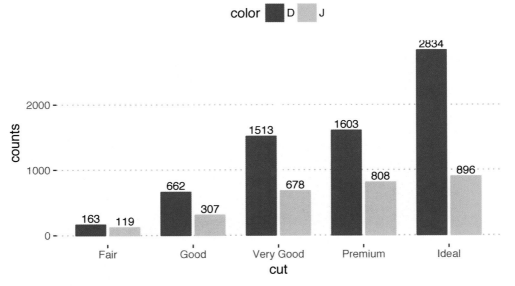

4. **Add labels to a stacked bar plots**. 3 steps required to compute the position of text labels:
   - Sort the data by cut and color columns. As `position_stack()` reverse the group order, `color` column should be sorted in descending order.
   - Calculate the cumulative sum of counts for each cut category. Used as the y coordinates of labels. To put the label in the middle of the bars, we'll use `cumsum(counts) - 0.5 * counts`.
   - Create the bar graph and add labels

```
# Arrange/sort and compute cumulative summs
df <- df %>%
  arrange(cut, desc(color)) %>%
  mutate(lab_ypos = cumsum(counts) - 0.5 * counts)
head(df, 4)
```

```
## # A tibble: 4 x 4
## # Groups:   cut [2]
##      cut color counts lab_ypos
##    <ord> <ord>  <int>    <dbl>
## 1  Fair     J     119     59.5
## 2  Fair     D     163    200.5
## 3  Good     J     307    153.5
## 4  Good     D     662    638.0
```

```
# Create stacked bar graphs with labels
ggplot(df, aes(x = cut, y = counts)) +
  geom_bar(aes(color = color, fill = color), stat = "identity") +
  geom_text(
    aes(y = lab_ypos, label = counts, group = color),
    color = "white"
  ) +
```

```
scale_color_manual(values = c("#0073C2FF", "#EFC000FF"))+
scale_fill_manual(values = c("#0073C2FF", "#EFC000FF"))
```

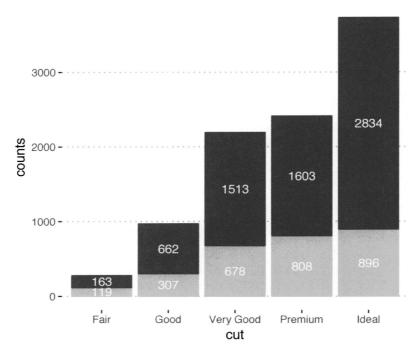

Alternatively, you can easily create the above plot using the function `ggbarplot()` [in ggpubr]:

```
ggbarplot(df, x = "cut", y = "counts",
          color = "color", fill = "color",
          palette = c("#0073C2FF", "#EFC000FF"),
          label = TRUE, lab.pos = "in", lab.col = "white",
          ggtheme = theme_pubclean()
          )
```

6. **Alternative to bar plots**. Instead of the creating a bar plot of the counts, you can plot two discrete variables with discrete x-axis and discrete y-axis. Each individual points are shown by groups. For a given group, the number of points corresponds to the number of records in that group.

Key function: `geom_jitter()`. Arguments: alpha, color, fill, shape and size.

In the example below, we'll plot a small fraction (1/5) of the diamonds dataset.

```
diamonds.frac <- dplyr::sample_frac(diamonds, 1/5)
ggplot(diamonds.frac, aes(cut, color)) +
  geom_jitter(aes(color = cut), size = 0.3)+
  ggpubr::color_palette("jco")+
```

```
ggpubr::theme_pubclean()
```

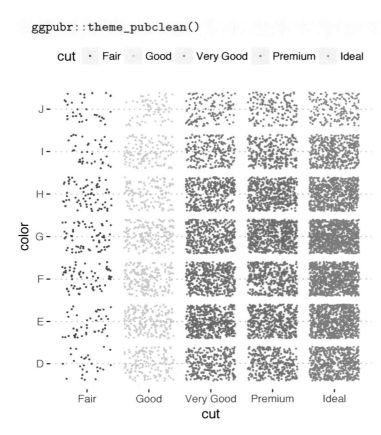

3.4 Grouped continuous variables

In this section, we'll show to plot a grouped continuous variable using box plot, violin plot, strip chart and alternatives.

We'll also describe how to add automatically p-values comparing groups.

In this section, we'll set the theme `theme_bw()` as the default ggplot theme:

```
theme_set(
  theme_bw()
)
```

3.4.1 Data format

- Demo dataset: `ToothGrowth`
  - Continuous variable: `len` (tooth length). Used on y-axis
  - Grouping variable: `dose` (dose levels of vitamin C: 0.5, 1, and 2 mg/day). Used on x-axis.

First, convert the variable `dose` from a numeric to a discrete factor variable:

```
data("ToothGrowth")
ToothGrowth$dose <- as.factor(ToothGrowth$dose)
head(ToothGrowth)
```

```
##      len supp dose
## 1   4.2   VC  0.5
## 2  11.5   VC  0.5
## 3   7.3   VC  0.5
## 4   5.8   VC  0.5
## 5   6.4   VC  0.5
## 6  10.0   VC  0.5
```

3.4.2   Box plots

- Key function: `geom_boxplot()`
- Key arguments to customize the plot:
  - `width`: the width of the box plot
  - `notch`: logical. If TRUE, creates a notched box plot. The notch displays a confidence interval around the median which is normally based on the `median +/- 1.58*IQR/sqrt(n)`. Notches are used to compare groups; if the notches of two boxes do not overlap, this is a strong evidence that the medians differ.
  - `color`, `size`, `linetype`: Border line color, size and type
  - `fill`: box plot areas fill color
  - `outlier.colour`, `outlier.shape`, `outlier.size`: The color, the shape and the size for outlying points.

1. **Create basic box plots**:

- Standard and notched box plots:

```
# Default plot
e <- ggplot(ToothGrowth, aes(x = dose, y = len))
e + geom_boxplot()

# Notched box plot with mean points
e + geom_boxplot(notch = TRUE, fill = "lightgray")+
  stat_summary(fun.y = mean, geom = "point",
               shape = 18, size = 2.5, color = "#FC4E07")
```

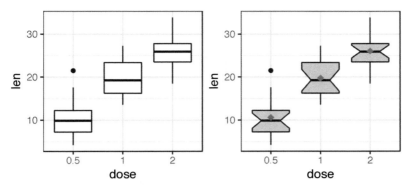

- Change box plot colors by groups:

```
# Color by group (dose)
e + geom_boxplot(aes(color = dose))+
  scale_color_manual(values = c("#00AFBB", "#E7B800", "#FC4E07"))
```

```
# Change fill color by group (dose)
e + geom_boxplot(aes(fill = dose)) +
  scale_fill_manual(values = c("#00AFBB", "#E7B800", "#FC4E07"))
```

Note that, it's possible to use the function `scale_x_discrete()` for:

- choosing which items to display: for example c("0.5", "2"),
- changing the order of items: for example from c("0.5", "1", "2") to c("2", "0.5", "1")

For example, type this:

```
# Choose which items to display: group "0.5" and "2"
e + geom_boxplot() +
  scale_x_discrete(limits=c("0.5", "2"))
```

```
# Change the default order of items
e + geom_boxplot() +
  scale_x_discrete(limits=c("2", "0.5", "1"))
```

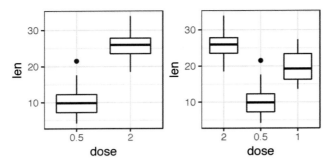

2. **Create a box plot with multiple groups**:

Two different grouping variables are used: `dose` on x-axis and `supp` as fill color (legend variable).

The space between the grouped box plots is adjusted using the function `position_dodge()`.

```
e2 <- e + geom_boxplot(
  aes(fill = supp),
  position = position_dodge(0.9)
  ) +
  scale_fill_manual(values = c("#999999", "#E69F00"))
e2
```

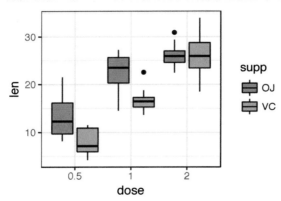

Split the plot into multiple panel. Use the function `facet_wrap()`:

```
e2 + facet_wrap(~supp)
```

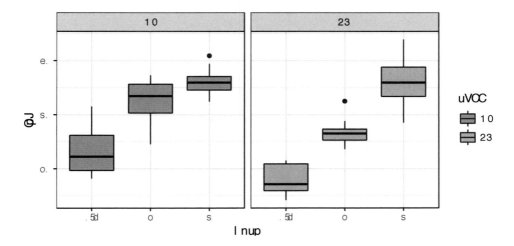

3.4.3 Violin plots

Violin plots are similar to box plots, except that they also show the kernel probability density of the data at different values. Typically, violin plots will include a marker for the median of the data and a box indicating the interquartile range, as in standard box plots.

Key function:

- `geom_violin()`: Creates violin plots. Key arguments:
    - `color`, `size`, `linetype`: Border line color, size and type
    - `fill`: Areas fill color
    - `trim`: logical value. If TRUE (default), trim the tails of the violins to the range of the data. If FALSE, don't trim the tails.
- `stat_summary()`: Adds summary statistics (mean, median, ...) on the violin plots.

1. **Create basic violin plots with summary statistics**:

```
# Add mean points +/- SD
# Use geom = "pointrange" or geom = "crossbar"
e + geom_violin(trim = FALSE) +
  stat_summary(
    fun.data = "mean_sdl",  fun.args = list(mult = 1),
    geom = "pointrange", color = "black"
    )


# Combine with box plot to add median and quartiles
# Change color by groups
e + geom_violin(aes(fill = dose), trim = FALSE) +
  geom_boxplot(width = 0.2)+
  scale_fill_manual(values = c("#00AFBB", "#E7B800", "#FC4E07"))+
  theme(legend.position = "none")
```

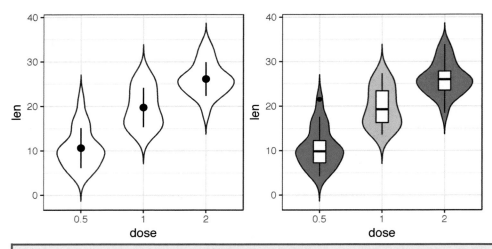

The function `mean_sdl` is used for adding mean and standard deviation. It computes the mean plus or minus a constant times the standard deviation. In the R code above, the constant is specified using the argument `mult` (mult = 1). By default mult = 2. The mean +/- SD can be added as a crossbar or a pointrange.

2. **Create violin plots with multiple groups**:

```
e + geom_violin(
  aes(color = supp), trim = FALSE,
  position = position_dodge(0.9)
  ) +
geom_boxplot(
    aes(color = supp), width = 0.15,
    position = position_dodge(0.9)
    ) +
scale_color_manual(values = c("#00AFBB", "#E7B800"))
```

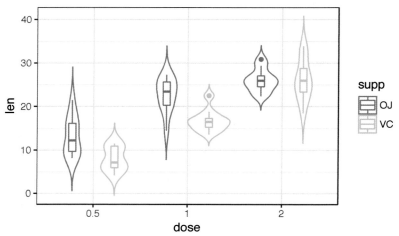

3.4.4 Dot plots

- Key function: `geom_dotplot()`. Creates stacked dots, with each dot representing one observation.
- Key arguments:
  - `stackdir`: which direction to stack the dots. "up" (default), "down", "center", "centerwhole" (centered, but with dots aligned).
  - `stackratio`: how close to stack the dots. Default is 1, where dots just just touch. Use smaller values for closer, overlapping dots.
  - `color`, `fill`: Dot border color and area fill
  - `dotsize`: The diameter of the dots relative to binwidth, default 1.

As for violin plots, summary statistics are usually added to dot plots.

1. **Create basic dot plots**:

```
# Violin plots with mean points +/- SD
e + geom_dotplot(
  binaxis = "y", stackdir = "center",
  fill = "lightgray"
  ) +
  stat_summary(
    fun.data = "mean_sdl", fun.args = list(mult=1),
    geom = "pointrange", color = "red"
    )


# Combine with box plots
e + geom_boxplot(width = 0.5) +
  geom_dotplot(
    binaxis = "y", stackdir = "center",
    fill = "white"
    )


# Dot plot + violin plot + stat summary
e + geom_violin(trim = FALSE) +
  geom_dotplot(
    binaxis='y', stackdir='center',
    color = "black", fill = "#999999"
    ) +
  stat_summary(
    fun.data="mean_sdl",  fun.args = list(mult=1),
    geom = "pointrange", color = "#FC4E07", size = 0.4
    )
```

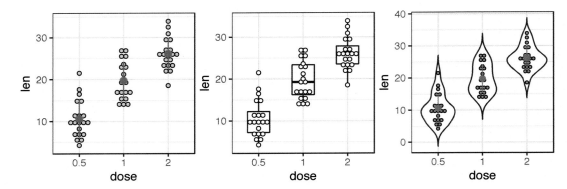

2. **Create dot plots with multiple groups:**

```
# Color dots by groups
e + geom_boxplot(width = 0.5, size = 0.4) +
  geom_dotplot(
    aes(fill = supp), trim = FALSE,
    binaxis='y', stackdir='center'
  )+
  scale_fill_manual(values = c("#00AFBB", "#E7B800"))

# Change the position : interval between dot plot of the same group
e + geom_boxplot(
  aes(color = supp), width = 0.5, size = 0.4,
  position = position_dodge(0.8)
  ) +
  geom_dotplot(
    aes(fill = supp, color = supp), trim = FALSE,
    binaxis='y', stackdir='center', dotsize = 0.8,
    position = position_dodge(0.8)
  )+
  scale_fill_manual(values = c("#00AFBB", "#E7B800"))+
  scale_color_manual(values = c("#00AFBB", "#E7B800"))
```

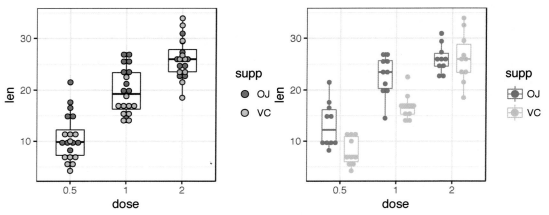

3.4.5   Stripcharts

Stripcharts are also known as one dimensional scatter plots. These plots are suitable compared to box plots when sample sizes are small.

- Key function: `geom_jitter()`
- key arguments: `color`, `fill`, `size`, `shape`. Changes points color, fill, size and shape

1. **Create a basic stripchart**:

- Change points shape and color by groups
- Adjust the degree of jittering: `position_jitter(0.2)`
- Add summary statistics:

```
e + geom_jitter(
  aes(shape = dose, color = dose),
  position = position_jitter(0.2),
  size = 1.2
  ) +
stat_summary(
  aes(color = dose),
  fun.data="mean_sdl",  fun.args = list(mult=1),
  geom = "pointrange",  size = 0.4
  )+
scale_color_manual(values =  c("#00AFBB", "#E7B800", "#FC4E07"))
```

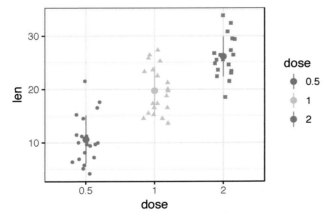

2. **Create stripcharts for multiple groups.** The R code is similar to what we have seen in dot plots section. However, to create dodged jitter points, you should use the function `position_jitterdodge()` instead of `position_dodge()`.

```
e + geom_jitter(
  aes(shape = supp, color = supp),
  position = position_jitterdodge(jitter.width = 0.2, dodge.width = 0.8),
  size = 1.2
  ) +
stat_summary(
```

```
    aes(color = supp),
    fun.data="mean_sdl",  fun.args = list(mult=1),
    geom = "pointrange",  size = 0.4,
    position = position_dodge(0.8)
    )+
scale_color_manual(values =  c("#00AFBB", "#E7B800"))
```

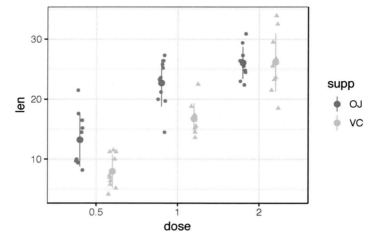

3.4.6   Sinaplot

sinaplot is inspired by the strip chart and the violin plot. By letting the normalized density of points restrict the jitter along the x-axis, the plot displays the same contour as a violin plot, but resemble a simple strip chart for small number of data points (Sidiropoulos et al., 2015).

In this way the plot conveys information of both the number of data points, the density distribution, outliers and spread in a very simple, comprehensible and condensed format.

Key function: `geom_sina()` [ggforce]:

```
library(ggforce)
# Create some data
d1 <- data.frame(
  y = c(rnorm(200, 4, 1), rnorm(200, 5, 2), rnorm(400, 6, 1.5)),
  group = rep(c("Grp1", "Grp2", "Grp3"), c(200, 200, 400))
  )

# Sinaplot
ggplot(d1, aes(group, y)) +
  geom_sina(aes(color = group), size = 0.7)+
  scale_color_manual(values =  c("#00AFBB", "#E7B800", "#FC4E07"))
```

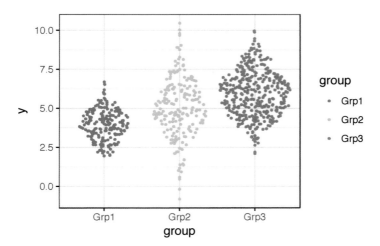

3.4.7 Mean and median plots with error bars

In this section, we'll show how to plot summary statistics of a continuous variable organized into groups by one or multiple grouping variables.

Note that, an easy way, with less typing, to create mean/median plots, is provided in the ggpubr package. See the associated article at: ggpubr-Plot Means/Medians and Error Bars[1]

Set the default theme to `theme_pubr()` [in ggpubr]:

```
theme_set(ggpubr::theme_pubr())
```

1. **Basic mean/median plots.** Case of one continuous variable and one grouping variable:

- Prepare the data: `ToothGrowth` data set.

```
df <- ToothGrowth
df$dose <- as.factor(df$dose)
head(df, 3)
```

```
##    len supp dose
## 1  4.2   VC  0.5
## 2 11.5   VC  0.5
## 3  7.3   VC  0.5
```

- Compute summary statistics for the variable `len` organized into groups by the variable `dose`:

```
library(dplyr)
df.summary <- df %>%
  group_by(dose) %>%
  summarise(
```

---

[1]http://www.sthda.com/english/articles/24-ggpubr-publication-ready-plots/

```
    sd = sd(len, na.rm = TRUE),
    len = mean(len)
  )
df.summary
```

```
## # A tibble: 3 x 3
##     dose     sd    len
##   <fctr> <dbl> <dbl>
## 1     0.5  4.50   10.6
## 2       1  4.42   19.7
## 3       2  3.77   26.1
```

- Create error plots using the summary statistics data. Key functions:
  - `geom_crossbar()` for hollow bar with middle indicated by horizontal line
  - `geom_errorbar()` for error bars
  - `geom_errorbarh()` for horizontal error bars
  - `geom_linerange()` for drawing an interval represented by a vertical line
  - `geom_pointrange()` for creating an interval represented by a vertical line, with a point in the middle.

Start by initializing ggplot with the summary statistics data:
- Specify x and y as usually - Specify `ymin = len-sd` and `ymax = len+sd` to add lower and upper error bars. If you want only to add upper error bars but not the lower ones, use `ymin = len` (instead of `len-sd`) and `ymax = len+sd`.

```
# Initialize ggplot with data
f <- ggplot(
  df.summary,
  aes(x = dose, y = len, ymin = len-sd, ymax = len+sd)
  )
```

Possible error plots:

f + geom_crossbar()   f + geom_errorbar()   f + geom_linerange()   f + geom_pointrange()

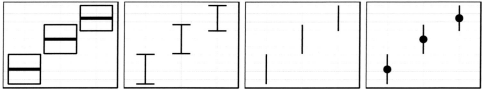

Create simple error plots:

```
# Vertical line with point in the middle
f + geom_pointrange()
```

```
# Standard error bars
f + geom_errorbar(width = 0.2) +
  geom_point(size = 1.5)
```

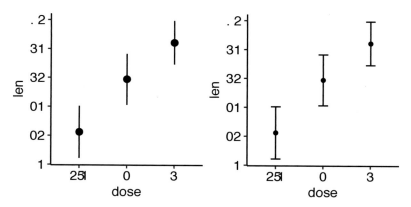

Create horizontal error bars. Put `dose` on y axis and `len` on x-axis. Specify `xmin` and `xmax`.

```
# Horizontal error bars with mean points
# Change the color by groups
ggplot(
  df.summary,
  aes(x = len, y = dose, xmin = len-sd, xmax = len+sd)
) +
  geom_point(aes(color = dose)) +
  geom_errorbarh(aes(color = dose), height=.2)+
  theme_light()
```

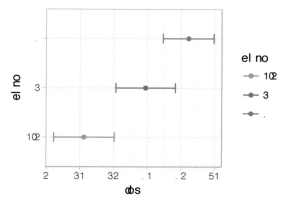

- Add jitter points (representing individual points), dot plots and violin plots. For this, you should initialize ggplot with original data (`df`) and specify the `df.summary` data in the error plot function, here `geom_pointrange()`.

```
# Combine with jitter points
ggplot(df, aes(dose, len)) +
  geom_jitter(
    position = position_jitter(0.2), color = "darkgray"
    ) +
  geom_pointrange(
    aes(ymin = len-sd, ymax = len+sd),
```

```
    data = df.summary
    )
```

```
# Combine with violin plots
ggplot(df, aes(dose, len)) +
  geom_violin(color = "darkgray", trim = FALSE) +
  geom_pointrange(
    aes(ymin = len-sd, ymax = len+sd),
    data = df.summary
    )
```

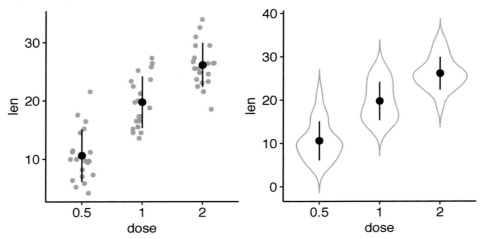

- Create basic bar/line plots of mean +/- error. So we need only the `df.summary` data.
  - (1) Add lower and upper error bars for the line plot: `ymin = len-sd` and `ymax = len+sd`.
  - (2) Add only upper error bars for the bar plot: `ymin = len` (instead of `len-sd`) and `ymax = len+sd`.

Note that, for line plot, you should always specify `group = 1` in the `aes()`, when you have one group of line.

```
# (1) Line plot
ggplot(df.summary, aes(dose, len)) +
  geom_line(aes(group = 1)) +
  geom_errorbar( aes(ymin = len-sd, ymax = len+sd),width = 0.2) +
  geom_point(size = 2)
```

```
# (2) Bar plot
ggplot(df.summary, aes(dose, len)) +
  geom_bar(stat = "identity", fill = "lightgray",
           color = "black") +
  geom_errorbar(aes(ymin = len, ymax = len+sd), width = 0.2)
```

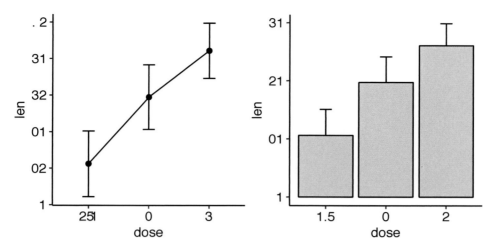

For line plot, you might want to treat x-axis as numeric:

```
df.sum2 <- df.summary
df.sum2$dose <- as.numeric(df.sum2$dose)
ggplot(df.sum2, aes(dose, len)) +
  geom_line() +
  geom_errorbar( aes(ymin = len-sd, ymax = len+sd),width = 0.2) +
  geom_point(size = 2)
```

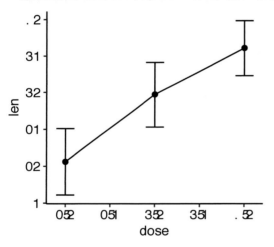

- Bar and line plots + jitter points. We need the original `df` data for the jitter points and the `df.summary` data for the other `geom` layers.
    - (1) For the line plot: First, add jitter points, then add lines + error bars + mean points on top of the jitter points.
    - (2) For the bar plot: First, add the bar plot, then add jitter points + error bars on top of the bars.

```
# (1) Create a line plot of means +
# individual jitter points + error bars
ggplot(df, aes(dose, len)) +
```

```
geom_jitter( position = position_jitter(0.2),
            color = "darkgray") +
geom_line(aes(group = 1), data = df.summary) +
geom_errorbar(
  aes(ymin = len-sd, ymax = len+sd),
  data = df.summary, width = 0.2) +
geom_point(data = df.summary, size = 2)

# (2) Bar plots of means + individual jitter points + errors
ggplot(df, aes(dose, len)) +
  geom_bar(stat = "identity", data = df.summary,
          fill = NA, color = "black") +
  geom_jitter( position = position_jitter(0.2),
              color = "black") +
  geom_errorbar(
    aes(ymin = len-sd, ymax = len+sd),
    data = df.summary, width = 0.2)
```

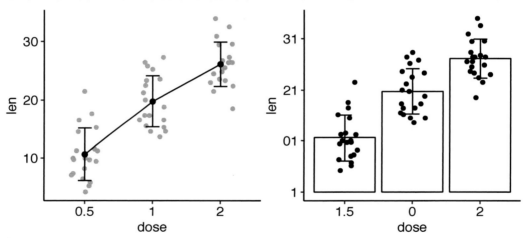

2. **Mean/median plots for multiple groups**. Case of one continuous variable
   (len) and two grouping variables (dose, supp).

- Compute the summary statistics of len grouped by dose and supp:

```
library(dplyr)
df.summary2 <- df %>%
  group_by(dose, supp) %>%
  summarise(
    sd = sd(len),
    len = mean(len)
  )
df.summary2

## # A tibble: 6 x 4
## # Groups:   dose [?]
```

```
##      dose    supp    sd    len
##    <fctr>  <fctr> <dbl> <dbl>
## 1    0.5      OJ  4.46 13.23
## 2    0.5      VC  2.75  7.98
## 3      1      OJ  3.91 22.70
## 4      1      VC  2.52 16.77
## 5      2      OJ  2.66 26.06
## 6      2      VC  4.80 26.14
```

- Create error plots for multiple groups:
    - (1) pointrange colored by groups (supp)
    - (2) standard error bars + mean points colored by groups (supp)

```
# (1) Pointrange: Vertical line with point in the middle
ggplot(df.summary2, aes(dose, len)) +
  geom_pointrange(
    aes(ymin = len-sd, ymax = len+sd, color = supp),
    position = position_dodge(0.3)
    )+
  scale_color_manual(values = c("#00AFBB", "#E7B800"))


# (2) Standard error bars
ggplot(df.summary2, aes(dose, len)) +
  geom_errorbar(
    aes(ymin = len-sd, ymax = len+sd, color = supp),
    position = position_dodge(0.3), width = 0.2
    )+
  geom_point(aes(color = supp), position = position_dodge(0.3)) +
  scale_color_manual(values = c("#00AFBB", "#E7B800"))
```

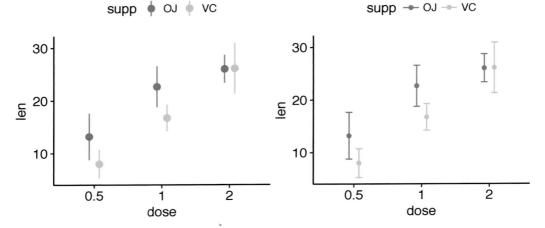

- Create simple line/bar plots for multiple groups.
    - (1) Line plots: change linetype by groups (supp)
    - (2) Bar plots: change fill color by groups (supp)

```
# (1) Line plot + error bars
ggplot(df.summary2, aes(dose, len)) +
  geom_line(aes(linetype = supp, group = supp))+
  geom_point()+
  geom_errorbar(
    aes(ymin = len-sd, ymax = len+sd, group = supp),
    width = 0.2
    )


# (2) Bar plots + upper error bars.
ggplot(df.summary2, aes(dose, len)) +
  geom_bar(aes(fill = supp), stat = "identity",
          position = position_dodge(0.8), width = 0.7)+
  geom_errorbar(
    aes(ymin = len, ymax = len+sd, group = supp),
    width = 0.2, position = position_dodge(0.8)
    )+
  scale_fill_manual(values = c("grey80", "grey30"))
```

- Create easily plots of mean +/- sd for multiple groups. Use the ggpubr package, which will automatically calculate the summary statistics and create the graphs.

```
library(ggpubr)
# Create line plots of means
ggline(ToothGrowth, x = "dose", y = "len",
       add = c("mean_sd", "jitter"),
       color = "supp", palette = c("#00AFBB", "#E7B800"))

# Create bar plots of means
ggbarplot(ToothGrowth, x = "dose", y = "len",
          add = c("mean_se", "jitter"),
          color = "supp", palette = c("#00AFBB", "#E7B800"),
          position = position_dodge(0.8))
```

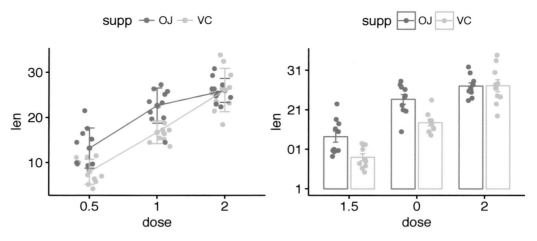

- Use the standard ggplot2 verbs, to reproduce the line plots above:

```
# Create line plots
ggplot(df, aes(dose, len)) +
  geom_jitter(
    aes(color = supp),
    position = position_jitter(0.2)
    ) +
  geom_line(
    aes(group = supp, color = supp),
    data = df.summary2
    ) +
  geom_errorbar(
    aes(ymin = len-sd, ymax = len+sd, color = supp),
    data = df.summary2, width = 0.2
    )+
  scale_color_manual(values = c("#00AFBB", "#E7B800"))
```

3.4.8   Add p-values and significance levels

In this section, we'll describe how to easily i) compare means of two or multiple groups; ii) and to automatically add p-values and significance levels to a ggplot (such as box plots, dot plots, bar plots and line plots, ...).

Key functions:

- `compare_means()` [ggpubr package]: easy to use solution to performs one and multiple mean comparisons.
- `stat_compare_means()` [ggpubr package]: easy to use solution to automatically add p-values and significance levels to a ggplot.

The most common methods for comparing means[2] include:

---

[2]http://www.sthda.com/english/wiki/comparing-means-in-r

Methods	R function	Description
T-test	t.test()	Compare two groups (parametric)
Wilcoxon test	wilcox.test()	Compare two groups (non-parametric)
ANOVA	aov() or anova()	Compare multiple groups (parametric)
Kruskal-Wallis	kruskal.test()	Compare multiple groups (non-parametric)

1. **Compare two independent groups**:

- Compute t-test:

```
library(ggpubr)
compare_means(len ~ supp, data = ToothGrowth,
              method = "t.test")
```

```
## # A tibble: 1 x 8
##     .y. group1 group2      p p.adj p.format p.signif method
##   <chr>  <chr>  <chr>  <dbl> <dbl>    <chr>    <chr>  <chr>
## 1   len     OJ     VC 0.0606 0.0606    0.061       ns T-test
```

- Create a box plot with p-values. Use the option `method = "t.test"` or `method = "wilcox.test"`. Default is wilcoxon test.

```
# Create a simple box plot and add p-values
p <- ggplot(ToothGrowth, aes(supp, len)) +
  geom_boxplot(aes(color = supp)) +
  scale_color_manual(values = c("#00AFBB", "#E7B800"))
p + stat_compare_means(method = "t.test")
```

```
# Display the significance level instead of the p-value
# Adjust label position
p + stat_compare_means(
  aes(label = ..p.signif..), label.x = 1.5, label.y = 40
  )
```

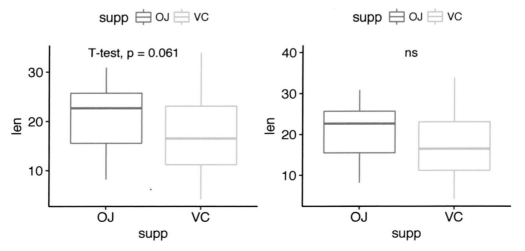

2. **Compare two paired samples**. Use `ggpaired()` [ggpubr] to create the paired

box plot.

```
ggpaired(ToothGrowth, x = "supp", y = "len",
         color = "supp", line.color = "gray", line.size = 0.4,
         palette = "jco")+
  stat_compare_means(paired = TRUE)
```

supp 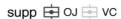 OJ VC

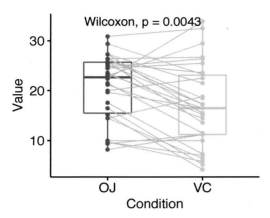

3. **Compare more than two groups**. If the grouping variable contains more than two levels, then pairwise tests will be performed automatically. The default method is "wilcox.test". You can change this to "t.test".

```
# Perorm pairwise comparisons
compare_means(len ~ dose,  data = ToothGrowth)
```

```
## # A tibble: 3 x 8
##      .y.  group1 group2        p   p.adj p.format p.signif    method
##    <chr>   <chr>  <chr>    <dbl>   <dbl>    <chr>    <chr>     <chr>
## 1   len     0.5      1 7.02e-06 1.40e-05  7.0e-06     **** Wilcoxon
## 2   len     0.5      2 8.41e-08 2.52e-07  8.4e-08     **** Wilcoxon
## 3   len       1      2 1.77e-04 1.77e-04  0.00018      *** Wilcoxon
```

```
# Visualize: Specify the comparisons you want
my_comparisons <- list( c("0.5", "1"), c("1", "2"), c("0.5", "2") )
ggboxplot(ToothGrowth, x = "dose", y = "len",
          color = "dose", palette = "jco")+
  stat_compare_means(comparisons = my_comparisons)+
  stat_compare_means(label.y = 50)
```

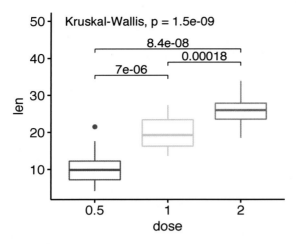

4. **Multiple grouping variables**:

- (1/2). Create a multi-panel box plots facetted by group (here, "dose"):

```
# Use only p.format as label. Remove method name.
ggplot(ToothGrowth, aes(supp, len)) +
  geom_boxplot(aes(color = supp))+
  facet_wrap(~dose) +
  scale_color_manual(values = c("#00AFBB", "#E7B800")) +
  stat_compare_means(label = "p.format")
```

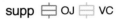

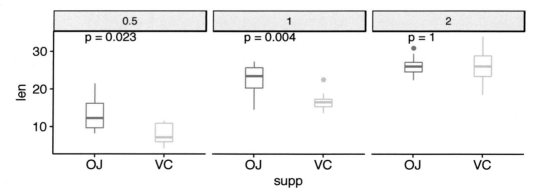

- (2/2). Create one single panel with all box plots. Plot y = "len" by x = "dose" and color by "supp". Specify the option group in stat_compare_means():

```
ggplot(ToothGrowth, aes(dose, len)) +
  geom_boxplot(aes(color = supp))+
  scale_color_manual(values = c("#00AFBB", "#E7B800")) +
  stat_compare_means(aes(group = supp), label = "p.signif")
```

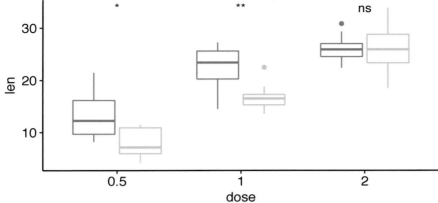

- Paired comparisons for multiple groups:

```r
# Box plot facetted by "dose"
p <- ggpaired(ToothGrowth, x = "supp", y = "len",
        color = "supp", palette = "jco",
        line.color = "gray", line.size = 0.4,
        facet.by = "dose", short.panel.labs = FALSE)
# Use only p.format as label. Remove method name.
p + stat_compare_means(label = "p.format", paired = TRUE)
```

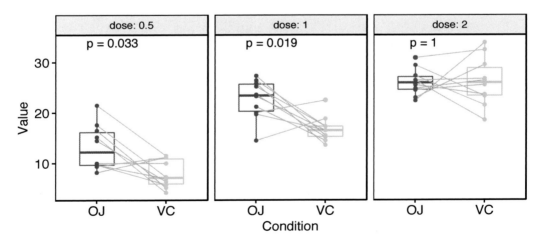

Read more at: Add P-values and Significance Levels to ggplots[3]

---

[3]http://www.sthda.com/english/articles/24-ggpubr-publication-ready-plots/76-add-p-values-and-significance-levels-to-ggplots/

3.5   Conclusion

1. **Visualize the distribution of a grouped continuous variable**: the grouping variable on x-axis and the continuous variable on y axis.

The possible ggplot2 layers include:

- `geom_boxplot()` for box plot
- `geom_violin()` for violin plot
- `geom_dotplot()` for dot plot
- `geom_jitter()` for stripchart
- `geom_line()` for line plot
- `geom_bar()` for bar plot

Examples of R code: start by creating a plot, named `e`, and then finish it by adding a layer:

```
ToothGrowth$dose <- as.factor(ToothGrowth$dose)
e <- ggplot(ToothGrowth, aes(x = dose, y = len))
```

2. **Create mean and median plots with error bars**: the grouping variable on x-axis and the summarized continuous variable (mean/median) on y-axis.

- Compute summary statistics and initialize ggplot with summary data:

```
# Summary statistics
library(dplyr)
df.summary <- ToothGrowth %>%
  group_by(dose) %>%
  summarise(
    sd = sd(len, na.rm = TRUE),
    len = mean(len)
  )
# Initialize ggplot with data
f <- ggplot(
```

```
df.summary,
aes(x = dose, y = len, ymin = len-sd, ymax = len+sd)
)
```

- Possible error plots:

f + geom_crossbar() **f + geom_errorbar()** **f + geom_linerange()** **f + geom_pointrange()**

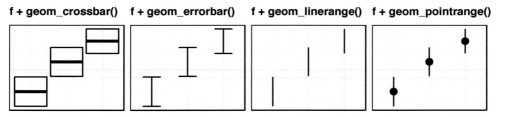

3. **Combine error bars with violin plots, dot plots, line and bar plots:**

```
# Combine with violin plots
ggplot(ToothGrowth, aes(dose, len))+
  geom_violin(trim = FALSE) +
  geom_pointrange(aes(ymin = len-sd, ymax = len + sd),
                  data = df.summary)

# Combine with dot plots
ggplot(ToothGrowth, aes(dose, len))+
  geom_dotplot(stackdir = "center", binaxis = "y",
               fill = "lightgray", dotsize = 1) +
  geom_pointrange(aes(ymin = len-sd, ymax = len + sd),
                  data = df.summary)

# Combine with line plot
ggplot(df.summary, aes(dose, len))+
  geom_line(aes(group = 1)) +
  geom_pointrange(aes(ymin = len-sd, ymax = len + sd))

# Combine with bar plots
ggplot(df.summary, aes(dose, len))+
  geom_bar(stat = "identity", fill = "lightgray") +
  geom_pointrange(aes(ymin = len-sd, ymax = len + sd))
```

3.6   See also

- ggpubr: Publication Ready Plots. https://goo.gl/7uySha
- Facilitating Exploratory Data Visualization: Application to TCGA Genomic Data. https://goo.gl/9LNsRi
- Add P-values and Significance Levels to ggplots. https://goo.gl/VH7Yq7
- Plot Means/Medians and Error Bars. https://goo.gl/zRwAeV

Chapter 4

Plot Two Continuous Variables

4.1 Introduction

Scatter plots are used to display the relationship between two continuous variables x and y. In this article, we'll start by showing how to create beautiful scatter plots in R.

We'll use helper functions in the ggpubr R package[1] to display automatically the **correlation coefficient** and the **significance level** on the plot.

We'll also describe how to color points by groups and to add concentration ellipses around each group. Additionally, we'll show how to create **bubble charts**, as well as, how to add **marginal plots** (histogram, density or box plot) to a scatter plot.

We continue by showing show some alternatives to the standard scatter plots, including rectangular binning, hexagonal binning and 2d density estimation. These plot types are useful in a situation where you have a large data set containing thousands of records.

R codes for zooming in scatter plot are also provided. Finally, you'll learn how to add fitted regression trend lines and equations to a scatter plot.

4.2 Prerequisites

1. **Install cowplot package**. Used to arrange multiple plots. Will be used here to create a scatter plot with marginal density plots. Install the latest developmental version as follow:

```
devtools::install_github("wilkelab/cowplot")
```

2. **Install ggpmisc** for adding the equation of a fitted regression line on a scatter plot:

```
install.packages("ggpmisc")
```

3. **Load required packages and set ggplot themes**:

---

[1]http://www.sthda.com/english/articles/24-ggpubr-publication-ready-plots/

68

- Load ggplot2 and ggpubr R packages
- Set the default theme to `theme_minimal()` [in ggplot2]

```
library(ggplot2)
library(ggpubr)
theme_set(
  theme_minimal() +
    theme(legend.position = "top")
)
```

4. **Prepare demo data sets**:

Dataset: mtcars[2]. The variable `cyl` is used as grouping variable.

```
# Load data
data("mtcars")
df <- mtcars

# Convert cyl as a grouping variable
df$cyl <- as.factor(df$cyl)

# Inspect the data
head(df[, c("wt", "mpg", "cyl", "qsec")], 4)
```

```
##                    wt  mpg cyl qsec
## Mazda RX4        2.62 21.0   6 16.5
## Mazda RX4 Wag    2.88 21.0   6 17.0
## Datsun 710       2.32 22.8   4 18.6
## Hornet 4 Drive   3.21 21.4   6 19.4
```

4.3 Basic scatter plots

Key functions:

- `geom_point()`: Create scatter plots. Key arguments: `color`, `size` and `shape` to change point color, size and shape.
- `geom_smooth()`: Add smoothed conditional means / regression line. Key arguments:
    - `color`, `size` and `linetype`: Change the line color, size and type.
    - `fill`: Change the fill color of the confidence region.

```
b <- ggplot(df, aes(x = wt, y = mpg))

# Scatter plot with regression line
b + geom_point()+
  geom_smooth(method = "lm")
```

---

[2]http://www.sthda.com/english/wiki/r-built-in-data-sets#mtcars-motor-trend-car-road-tests

```
# Add a loess smoothed fit curve
b + geom_point()+
  geom_smooth(method = "loess")
```

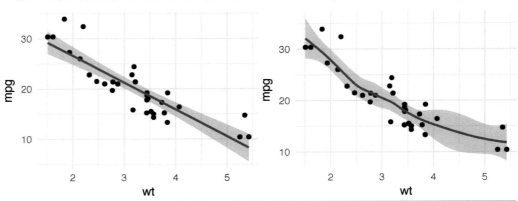

> To remove the confidence region around the regression line, specify the argument **se** = FALSE in the function **geom_smooth()**.

Change the point shape, by specifying the argument **shape**, for example:

```
b + geom_point(shape = 18)
```

To see the different point shapes commonly used in R, type this:

```
ggpubr::show_point_shapes()
```

Point shapes available in R

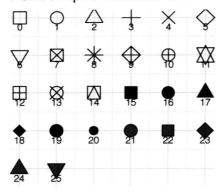

Create easily a scatter plot using **ggscatter()** [in ggpubr]. Use **stat_cor()** [ggpubr] to add the correlation coefficient and the significance level.

```
# Add regression line and confidence interval
# Add correlation coefficient: stat_cor()
ggscatter(df, x = "wt", y = "mpg",
          add = "reg.line", conf.int = TRUE,
          add.params = list(fill = "lightgray"),
          ggtheme = theme_minimal()
```

```
        )+
stat_cor(method = "pearson",
        label.x = 3, label.y = 30)
```

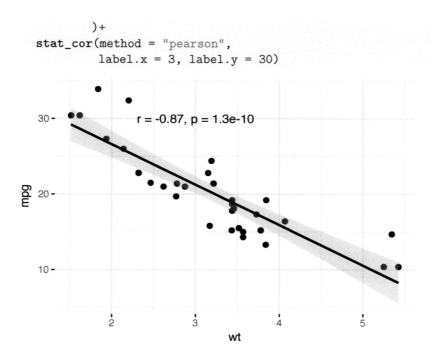

4.4 Multiple groups

- Change point colors and shapes by groups.
- Add marginal rug: geom_rug().

```
# Change color and shape by groups (cyl)
b + geom_point(aes(color = cyl, shape = cyl))+
  geom_smooth(aes(color = cyl, fill = cyl), method = "lm") +
  geom_rug(aes(color =cyl)) +
  scale_color_manual(values = c("#00AFBB", "#E7B800", "#FC4E07"))+
  scale_fill_manual(values = c("#00AFBB", "#E7B800", "#FC4E07"))

# Remove confidence region (se = FALSE)
# Extend the regression lines: fullrange = TRUE
b + geom_point(aes(color = cyl, shape = cyl)) +
  geom_rug(aes(color =cyl)) +
  geom_smooth(aes(color = cyl), method = lm,
            se = FALSE, fullrange = TRUE)+
  scale_color_manual(values = c("#00AFBB", "#E7B800", "#FC4E07"))+
  ggpubr::stat_cor(aes(color = cyl), label.x = 3)
```

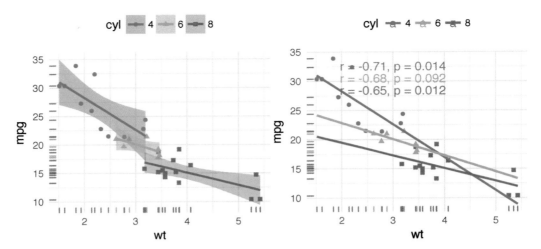

- Split the plot into multiple panels. Use the function `facet_wrap()`:

```
b + geom_point(aes(color = cyl, shape = cyl))+
  geom_smooth(aes(color = cyl, fill = cyl),
              method = "lm", fullrange = TRUE) +
  facet_wrap(~cyl) +
  scale_color_manual(values = c("#00AFBB", "#E7B800", "#FC4E07"))+
  scale_fill_manual(values = c("#00AFBB", "#E7B800", "#FC4E07")) +
  theme_bw()
```

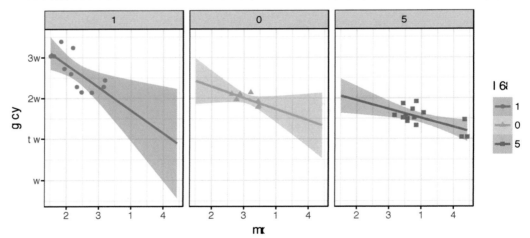

- Add concentration ellipse around groups. R function `stat_ellipse()`. Key arguments:
  - `type`: The type of ellipse. The default "t" assumes a multivariate t-distribution, and "norm" assumes a multivariate normal distribution. "euclid" draws a circle with the radius equal to level, representing the euclidean distance from the center.
  - `level`: The confidence level at which to draw an ellipse (default is 0.95), or, if type="euclid", the radius of the circle to be drawn.

```
b + geom_point(aes(color = cyl, shape = cyl))+
  stat_ellipse(aes(color = cyl), type = "t")+
  scale_color_manual(values = c("#00AFBB", "#E7B800", "#FC4E07"))
```

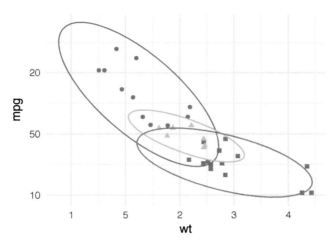

Instead of drawing the concentration ellipse, you can: i) plot a convex hull of a set of points; ii) add the mean points and the confidence ellipse of each group. Key R functions: stat_chull(), stat_conf_ellipse() and stat_mean() [in ggpubr]:

```
# Convex hull of groups
b + geom_point(aes(color = cyl, shape = cyl)) +
  stat_chull(aes(color = cyl, fill = cyl),
             alpha = 0.1, geom = "polygon") +
  scale_color_manual(values = c("#00AFBB", "#E7B800", "#FC4E07")) +
  scale_fill_manual(values = c("#00AFBB", "#E7B800", "#FC4E07"))

# Add mean points and confidence ellipses
b + geom_point(aes(color = cyl, shape = cyl)) +
  stat_conf_ellipse(aes(color = cyl, fill = cyl),
                    alpha = 0.1, geom = "polygon") +
  stat_mean(aes(color = cyl, shape = cyl), size = 2) +
  scale_color_manual(values = c("#00AFBB", "#E7B800", "#FC4E07")) +
  scale_fill_manual(values = c("#00AFBB", "#E7B800", "#FC4E07"))
```

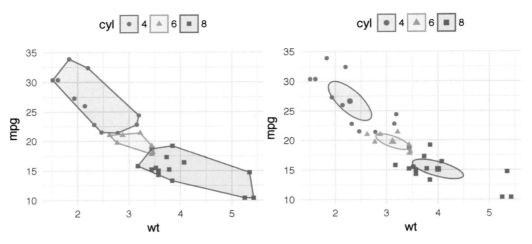

- Easy alternative using **ggpubr**. See this article: Perfect Scatter Plots with Correlation and Marginal Histograms[3]

```
# Add group mean points and stars
ggscatter(df, x = "wt", y = "mpg",
          color = "cyl", palette = "npg",
          shape = "cyl", ellipse = TRUE,
          mean.point = TRUE, star.plot = TRUE,
          ggtheme = theme_minimal())
```

```
# Change the ellipse type to 'convex'
ggscatter(df, x = "wt", y = "mpg",
          color = "cyl", palette = "npg",
          shape = "cyl",
          ellipse = TRUE, ellipse.type = "convex",
          ggtheme = theme_minimal())
```

[3]http://www.sthda.com/english/articles/24-ggpubr-publication-ready-plots/79-plot-meansmedians-and-error-bars/

4.5 Add point text labels

Key functions:

- `geom_text()` and `geom_label()`: ggplot2 standard functions to add text to a plot.
- `geom_text_repel()` and `geom_label_repel()` [in ggrepel package]. Repulsive textual annotations. Avoid text overlapping.

First install **ggrepel** (`install.packages("ggrepel")`), then type this:

```
library(ggrepel)
```

```
# Add text to the plot
.labs <- rownames(df)
b + geom_point(aes(color = cyl)) +
  geom_text_repel(aes(label = .labs,  color = cyl), size = 3)+
  scale_color_manual(values = c("#00AFBB", "#E7B800", "#FC4E07"))
```

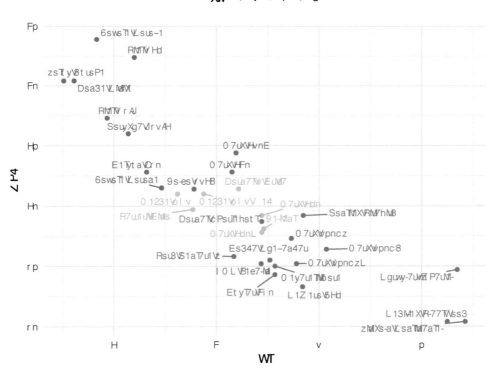

```
# Draw a rectangle underneath the text, making it easier to read.
b + geom_point(aes(color = cyl)) +
  geom_label_repel(aes(label = .labs,  color = cyl), size = 3)+
  scale_color_manual(values = c("#00AFBB", "#E7B800", "#FC4E07"))
```

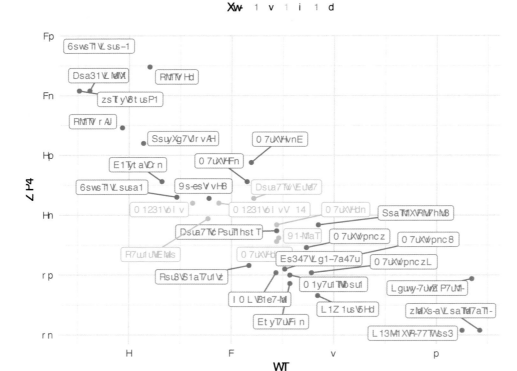

4.6   Bubble chart

In a bubble chart, points `size` is controlled by a continuous variable, here `qsec`. In the
R code below, the argument alpha is used to control color transparency. alpha should be
between 0 and 1.

```
b + geom_point(aes(color = cyl, size = qsec), alpha = 0.5) +
  scale_color_manual(values = c("#00AFBB", "#E7B800", "#FC4E07")) +
  scale_size(range = c(0.5, 12))  # Adjust the range of points size
```

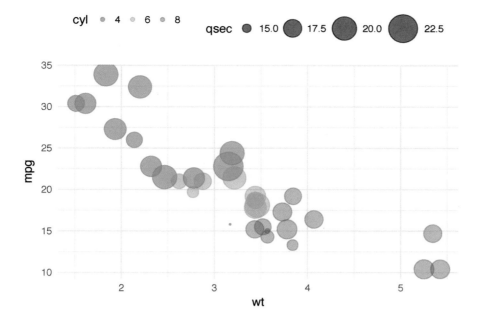

4.7 Color by a continuous variable

- Color points according to the values of the continuous variable: "mpg".
- Change the default blue gradient color using the function `scale_color_gradientn()` [in ggplot2], by specifying two or more colors.

```
b + geom_point(aes(color = mpg), size = 3) +
  scale_color_gradientn(colors = c("#00AFBB", "#E7B800", "#FC4E07"))
```

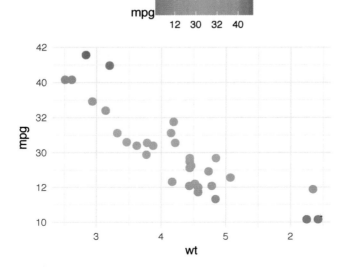

4.8   Add marginal density plots

The function `ggMarginal()` [in ggExtra package] (Attali, 2017), can be used to easily add a marginal histogram, density or box plot to a scatter plot.

First, install the ggExtra package as follow: `install.packages("ggExtra")`; then type the following R code:

```
# Create a scatter plot
p <- ggplot(iris, aes(Sepal.Length, Sepal.Width)) +
  geom_point(aes(color = Species), size = 3, alpha = 0.6) +
  scale_color_manual(values = c("#00AFBB", "#E7B800", "#FC4E07"))

# Add density distribution as marginal plot
library("ggExtra")
ggMarginal(p, type = "density")

# Change marginal plot type
ggMarginal(p, type = "boxplot")
```

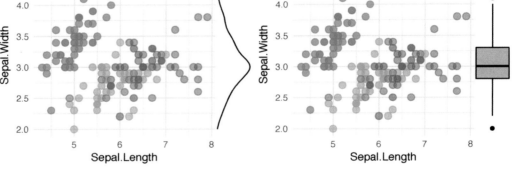

One limitation of ggExtra is that it can't cope with multiple groups in the scatter plot and the marginal plots.

A solution is provided in the function `ggscatterhist()` [ggpubr]:

```
library(ggpubr)
# Grouped Scatter plot with marginal density plots
ggscatterhist(
  iris, x = "Sepal.Length", y = "Sepal.Width",
  color = "Species", size = 3, alpha = 0.6,
  palette = c("#00AFBB", "#E7B800", "#FC4E07"),
  margin.params = list(fill = "Species", color = "black", size = 0.2)
  )
```

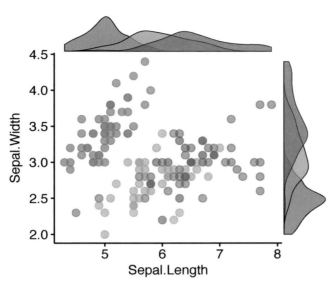

```
# Use box plot as marginal plots
ggscatterhist(
  iris, x = "Sepal.Length", y = "Sepal.Width",
  color = "Species", size = 3, alpha = 0.6,
  palette = c("#00AFBB", "#E7B800", "#FC4E07"),
  margin.plot = "boxplot",
  ggtheme = theme_bw()
  )
```

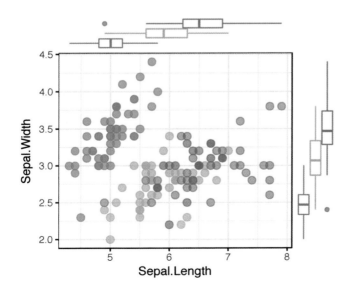

4.9   Continuous bivariate distribution

In this section, we'll present some alternatives to the standard scatter plots. These include:

- Rectangular binning. Rectangular heatmap of 2d bin counts
- Hexagonal binning: Hexagonal heatmap of 2d bin counts.
- 2d density estimation

1. **Rectangular binning**:

Rectangular binning is a very useful alternative to the standard scatter plot in a situation where you have a large data set containing thousands of records.

Rectangular binning helps to handle overplotting. Rather than plotting each point, which would appear highly dense, it divides the plane into rectangles, counts the number of cases in each rectangle, and then plots a heatmap of 2d bin counts. In this plot, many small hexagon are drawn with a color intensity corresponding to the number of cases in that bin.

Key function: `geom_bin2d()`: Creates a heatmap of 2d bin counts. Key arguments: `bins`, numeric vector giving number of bins in both vertical and horizontal directions. Set to 30 by default.

2. **Hexagonal binning**: Similar to rectangular binning, but divides the plane into regular hexagons. Hexagon bins avoid the visual artefacts sometimes generated by the very regular alignment of 'geom_bin2d().

Key function: `geom_hex()`

3. **Contours of a 2d density estimate**. Perform a 2D kernel density estimation and display results as contours overlaid on the scatter plot. This can be also useful for dealing with overplotting.

Key function: `geom_density_2d()`

- **Create a scatter plot with rectangular and hexagonal binning**:

```
# Rectangular binning
ggplot(diamonds, aes(carat, price)) +
  geom_bin2d(bins = 20, color ="white")+
  scale_fill_gradient(low =  "#00AFBB", high = "#FC4E07")+
  theme_minimal()

# Hexagonal binning
ggplot(diamonds, aes(carat, price)) +
  geom_hex(bins = 20, color = "white")+
  scale_fill_gradient(low =  "#00AFBB", high = "#FC4E07")+
  theme_minimal()
```

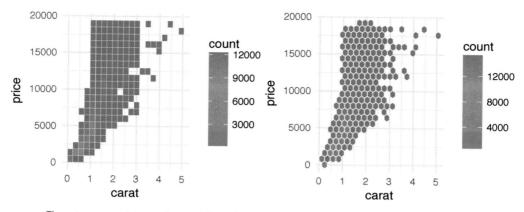

- **Create a scatter plot with 2d density estimation:**

```
# Add 2d density estimation
sp <- ggplot(iris, aes(Sepal.Length, Sepal.Width)) +
  geom_point(color = "lightgray")
sp + geom_density_2d()
```

```
# Use different geometry and change the gradient color
sp + stat_density_2d(aes(fill = ..level..), geom = "polygon") +
  scale_fill_gradientn(colors = c("#FFEDA0", "#FEB24C", "#F03B20"))
```

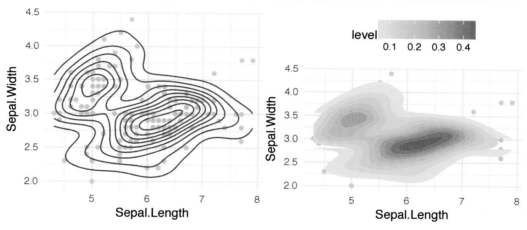

4.10   Zoom in a scatter plot

- Key function: `facet_zomm()` [in ggforce] (Pedersen, 2016).
- Demo data set: `iris`. The R code below zoom the points where `Species == "versicolor"`.

```
library(ggforce)
ggplot(iris, aes(Petal.Length, Petal.Width, colour = Species)) +
  geom_point() +
```

```
ggpubr::color_palette("jco") +
facet_zoom(x = Species == "versicolor")+
theme_bw()
```

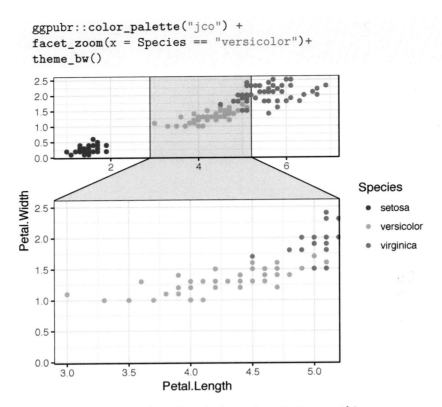

To zoom the points, where `Petal.Length < 2.5`, type this:

```
ggplot(iris, aes(Petal.Length, Petal.Width, colour = Species)) +
  geom_point() +
  ggpubr::color_palette("jco") +
  facet_zoom(x = Petal.Length < 2.5)+
  theme_bw()
```

4.11   Add trend lines and equations

In this section, we'll describe how to add trend lines to a scatter plot and labels (equation, R2, BIC, AIC) for a fitted lineal model.

    1. **Load packages and create a basic scatter plot facetted by groups:**

```
# Load packages and set theme
library(ggpubr)
library(ggpmisc)

theme_set(
  theme_bw() +
    theme(legend.position = "top")
  )
```

```
# Scatter plot
p <- ggplot(iris, aes(Sepal.Length, Sepal.Width)) +
  geom_point(aes(color = Species), size = 3, alpha = 0.6) +
  scale_color_manual(values = c("#00AFBB", "#E7B800", "#FC4E07")) +
  scale_fill_manual(values = c("#00AFBB", "#E7B800", "#FC4E07"))+
  facet_wrap(~Species)
```

2. **Add regression line, correlation coefficient and equantions of the fitted line**. Key functions:
   - stat_smooth() [ggplot2]
   - stat_cor() [ggpubr]
   - stat_poly_eq()[ggpmisc]

```
formula <- y ~ x
p +
  stat_smooth( aes(color = Species, fill = Species), method = "lm") +
  stat_cor(aes(color = Species), label.y = 4.4)+
  stat_poly_eq(
    aes(color = Species, label = ..eq.label..),
    formula = formula, label.y = 4.2, parse = TRUE)
```

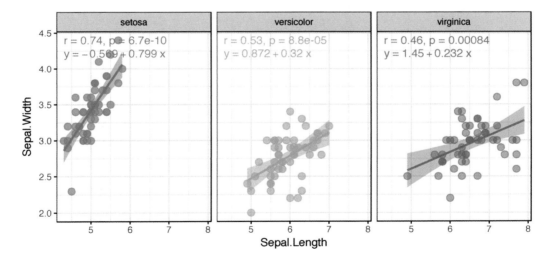

3. **Fit polynomial equation**:

- Create some data:

```
set.seed(4321)
x <- 1:100
y <- (x + x^2 + x^3) + rnorm(length(x), mean = 0, sd = mean(x^3) / 4)
my.data <- data.frame(x, y, group = c("A", "B"),
                      y2 = y * c(0.5,2), block = c("a", "a", "b", "b"))
```

- Fit polynomial regression line and add labels:

```
# Polynomial regression. Sow equation and adjusted R2
formula <- y ~ poly(x, 3, raw = TRUE)
p <- ggplot(my.data, aes(x, y2, color = group)) +
  geom_point() +
  geom_smooth(aes(fill = group), method = "lm", formula = formula) +
  stat_poly_eq(
    aes(label =  paste(..eq.label.., ..adj.rr.label.., sep = "~~~~")),
    formula = formula, parse = TRUE
    )
ggpar(p, palette = "jco")
```

group  A   B

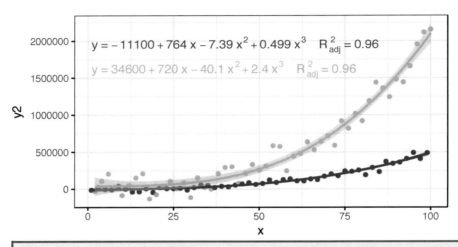

Note that, you can also display the AIC and the BIC values using ..AIC.label..
and ..BIC.label.. in the above equation.

Other arguments (label.x, label.y) are available in the function stat_poly_eq() to
adjust label positions.

For more examples, type this R code: browseVignettes("ggpmisc").

4.12   Conclusion

1. Create a basic scatter plot:

```
b <- ggplot(mtcars, aes(x = wt, y = mpg))
```

Possible layers, include:

- geom_point() for scatter plot
- geom_smooth() for adding smoothed line such as regression line
- geom_rug() for adding a marginal rug
- geom_text() for adding textual annotations

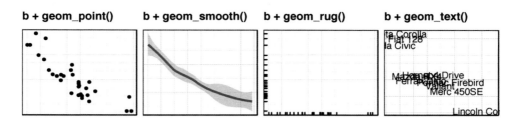

2. Continuous bivariate distribution:

```
c <- ggplot(diamonds, aes(carat, price))
```

Possible layers include:

- `geom_bin2d()`: Rectangular binning.
- `geom_hex()`: Hexagonal binning.
- `geom_density_2d()`: Contours from a 2d density estimate

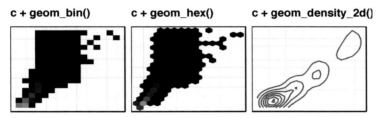

4.13   See also

- ggpubr: Publication Ready Plots. `https://goo.gl/7uySha`
- Perfect Scatter Plots with Correlation and Marginal Histograms. `https://goo.gl/3o4ddg`

Chapter 5

Plot Multivariate Continuous Data

5.1 Introduction

Here, multivariate data are data that contains 3 or more variables.

When you have only three continuous variables in your data set, you can create a **3d scatter plot**.

For a small data set with more than three variables, it's possible to visualize the relationship between each pairs of variables by creating a **scatter plot matrix**. You can also perform a correlation analysis between each pairs of variables.

For a large multivariate data set, it is more difficult to visualize their relationships. Discovering knowledge from these data requires specific techniques. **Multivariate analysis (MVA)** refers to a set of techniques used for analyzing a data set containing multiple variables.

Among these techniques, there are:

- Cluster analysis[1] for identifying groups of observations with similar profile according to a specific criteria.
- Principal component methods[2], which consist of summarizing and visualizing the most important information contained in a multivariate data set.

In this chapter we provide an overview of methods for visualizing multivariate data sets.

5.2 Demo data set and R package

```
library("magrittr") # for piping %>%
head(iris, 3)
```

```
##   Sepal.Length Sepal.Width Petal.Length Petal.Width Species
```

---

[1]http://www.sthda.com/english/articles/25-cluster-analysis-in-r-practical-guide/

[2]http://www.sthda.com/english/articles/31-principal-component-methods-in-r-practical-guide/

```
## 1        5.1        3.5        1.4        0.2  setosa
## 2        4.9        3.0        1.4        0.2  setosa
## 3        4.7        3.2        1.3        0.2  setosa
```

5.3 Create a 3d scatter plot

You can create a 3d scatter plot using the R package **scatterplot3d** (Ligges et al., 2017), which contains a function of the same name.

- Install: `install.packages("scatterplot3d")`

- Create a basic 3d scatter plot:

```
library(scatterplot3d)
scatterplot3d(
  iris[,1:3], pch = 19, color = "steelblue",
  grid = TRUE, box = FALSE,
  mar = c(3, 3, 0.5, 3)
  )
```

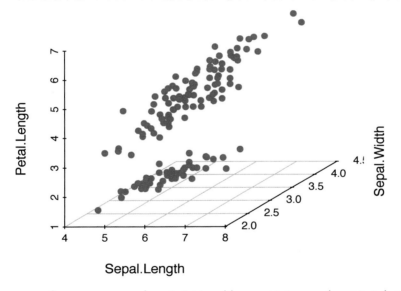

- See more examples at: http://www.sthda.com/english/wiki/3d-graphics

5.4 Create a scatter plot matrix

To create a scatter plot of each possible pairs of variables, you can use the function **ggpairs**() [in `GGally` package, an extension of ggplot2](Schloerke et al., 2016) . It produces a pairwise comparison of multivariate data.

- Install: `install.packages("GGally")`

- Create a simple scatter plot matrix. The plot contains the:
  - Scatter plot and the correlation coefficient between each pair of variables
  - Density distribution of each variable

```
library(GGally)
library(ggplot2)
ggpairs(iris[,-5])+ theme_bw()
```

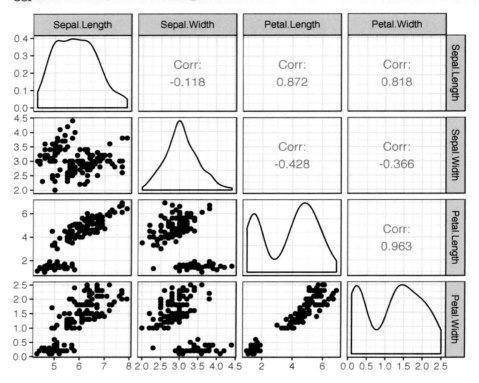

- Create a scatter plot matrix by groups. The plot contains the :
  - Scatter plot and the correlation coefficient, between each pair of variables, colored by groups
  - Density distribution and the box plot, of each continuous variable, colored by groups

```
p <- ggpairs(iris, aes(color = Species))+ theme_bw()
# Change color manually.
# Loop through each plot changing relevant scales
for(i in 1:p$nrow) {
  for(j in 1:p$ncol){
    p[i,j] <- p[i,j] +
        scale_fill_manual(values=c("#00AFBB", "#E7B800", "#FC4E07")) +
        scale_color_manual(values=c("#00AFBB", "#E7B800",` "#FC4E07"))
  }
}
p
```

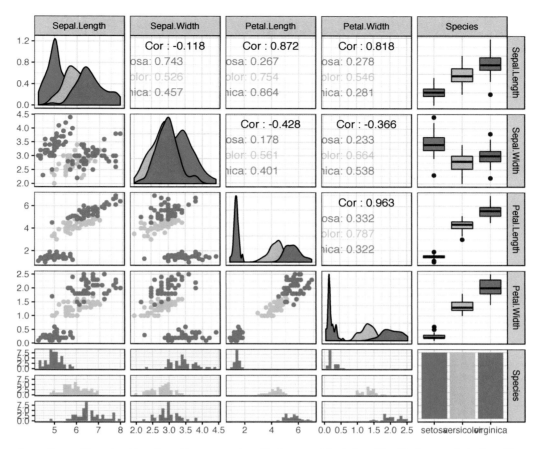

An alternative to the function **ggpairs()** is provided by the R base plot function **chart.Correlation()** [in PerformanceAnalytics packages]. It displays the correlation coefficient and the significance levels as stars.

For example, type the following R code, after installing the **PerformanceAnalytics** package:

```
# install.packages("PerformanceAnalytics")
library("PerformanceAnalytics")
my_data <- mtcars[, c(1,3,4,5,6,7)]
chart.Correlation(my_data, histogram=TRUE, pch=19)
```

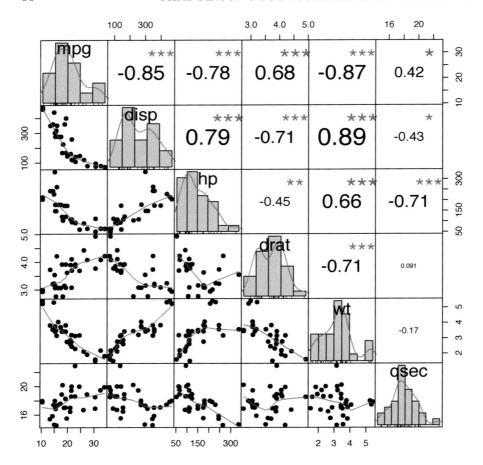

5.5   Correlation analysis

Recall that, correlation analysis is used to investigate the association between two or more variables. Read more at: Correlation analyses in R[3].

1. Compute correlation matrix between pairs of variables using the R base function `cor()`
2. Visualize the output. Two possibilities:
   - Use the function `ggcorrplot()` [in ggcorplot package]. Extension to the ggplot2 system. See more examples at: `http://www.sthda.com/english/wiki/ggcorrplot-visualization-of-a-correlation-matrix-using-ggplot2`.
   - Use the function `corrplot()` [in corrplot package]. R base plotting system. See examples at: `http://www.sthda.com/english/wiki/visualize-correlation-matrix-using-correlogram`.

Here, we'll present only the `ggcorrplot` package (Kassambara, 2016), which can be installed as follow: `install.packages("ggcorrplot")`.

---

[3]`http://www.sthda.com/english/wiki/correlation-analyses-in-r`

```r
library("ggcorrplot")
# Compute a correlation matrix
my_data <- mtcars[, c(1,3,4,5,6,7)]
corr <- round(cor(my_data), 1)
# Visualize
ggcorrplot(corr, p.mat = cor_pmat(my_data),
           hc.order = TRUE, type = "lower",
           color = c("#FC4E07", "white", "#00AFBB"),
           outline.col = "white", lab = TRUE)
```

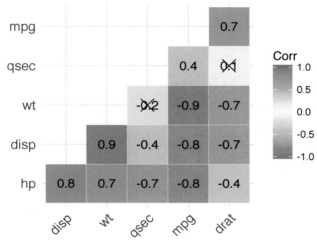

In the plot above:

- Positive correlations are shown in blue and negative correlation in red
- Variables that are associated are grouped together.
- Non-significant correlation are marked by a cross (X)

5.6 Principal component analysis

Principal component analysis (PCA) is a multivariate data analysis approach that allows us to summarize and visualize the most important information contained in a multivariate data set.

PCA reduces the data into few new dimensions (or axes), which are a linear combination of the original variables. You can visualize a multivariate data by drawing a scatter plot of the first two dimensions, which contain the most important information in the data. Read more at: https://goo.gl/kabVHq

- Demo data set: `iris`
- Compute PCA using the R base function `prcomp()`
- Visualize the output using the `factoextra` R package (an extension to ggplot2) (Kassambara and Mundt, 2017)

```
library("factoextra")
my_data <- iris[, -5] # Remove the grouping variable
res.pca <- prcomp(my_data, scale = TRUE)
fviz_pca_biplot(res.pca, col.ind = iris$Species,
                palette = "jco", geom = "point")
```

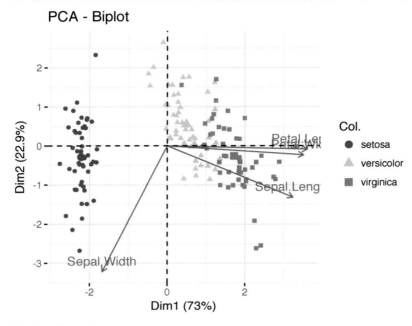

In the plot above:

- Dimension (Dim.) 1 and 2 retained about 96% (73% + 22.9%) of the total information contained in the data set.
- Individuals with a similar profile are grouped together
- Variables that are positively correlated are on the same side of the plots. Variables that are negatively correlated are on the opposite side of the plots.

5.7   Cluster analysis

Cluster analysis is one of the important data mining methods for discovering knowledge in multidimensional data. The goal of clustering is to identify pattern or groups of similar objects within a data set of interest. Read more at: http://www.sthda.com/english/articles/25-cluster-analysis-in-r-practical-guide/.

This section describes how to compute and visualize hierarchical clustering, which output is a tree called dendrogram showing groups of similar individuals.

- Computation. R function: hclust(). It takes a dissimilarity matrix as an input, which is calculated using the function dist().
- Visualization: fviz_dend() [in factoextra]
- Demo data sets: USArrests

Before cluster analysis, it's recommended to scale (or normalize) the data, to make the variables comparable. R function: `scale()`, applies scaling on the column of the data (variables).

```
library(factoextra)
USArrests %>%
  scale() %>%                           # Scale the data
  dist() %>%                            # Compute distance matrix
  hclust(method = "ward.D2") %>%        # Hierarchical clustering
  fviz_dend(cex = 0.5, k = 4, palette = "jco") # Visualize and cut
                                                # into 4 groups
```

Cluster Dendrogram

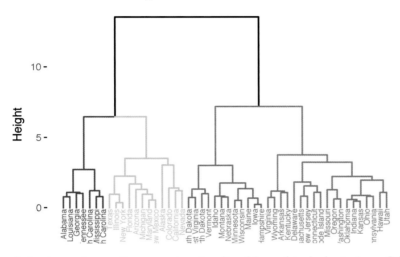

A heatmap is another way to visualize hierarchical clustering. It's also called a false colored image, where data values are transformed to color scale. Heat maps allow us to simultaneously visualize groups of samples and features. You can easily create a pretty heatmap using the R package `pheatmap`.

In heatmap, generally, columns are samples and rows are variables. Therefore we start by scaling and then transpose the data before creating the heatmap.

```
library(pheatmap)
USArrests %>%
  scale() %>%                # Scale variables
  t() %>%                    # Transpose
  pheatmap(cutree_cols = 4)  # Create the heatmap
```

5.8   Conclusion

For a multivariate continuous data, you can perform the following analysis or visualization depending on the complexity of your data:

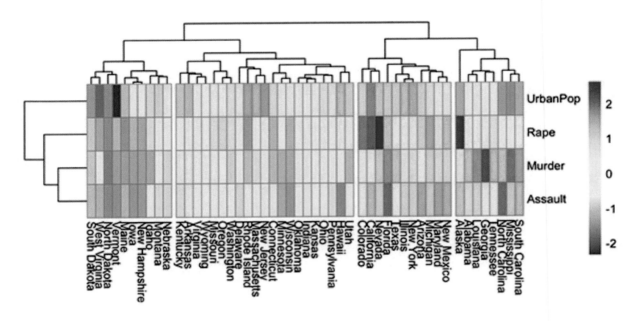

Figure 5.1: Multivariate data Heatmap

- 3D scatter plot : scatterplot3d() [scatterplot3d]
- Create a scatter plot matrix: ggpairs [GGally]
- Correlation matrix analysis and visualization: cor()[stats] and ggcorrplot() [ggcorrplot] for the visualization.
- Principal component analysis: prcomp() [stats] and fviz_pca() [factoextra]
- Cluster analysis: hclust() [stats] and fviz_dend() [factoextra]

Chapter 6

Visualizing Multivariate Categorical Data

6.1 Introduction

To visualize a small data set containing multiple categorical variables, you can create either a bar plot, a balloon plot or a mosaic plot.

For a large multivariate categorical data, you need specialized techniques dedicated to categorical data analysis, such as simple and multiple correspondence analysis[1]. These methods make it possible to visualize the association between a large number of categorical variables.

Here, we'll describe simple examples of graphs for visualizing the frequency distribution of categorical variables contained in small contingency tables.

6.2 Prerequisites

Load required R packages and set the default theme:

```
library(ggplot2)
library(ggpubr)
theme_set(theme_pubr())
```

6.3 Bar plots of contingency tables

Demo data set: `HairEyeColor` (distribution of hair and eye color and sex in 592 statistics students)

- Prepare and inspect the data:

---

[1]http://www.sthda.com/english/articles/31-principal-component-methods-in-r-practical-guide/

```
data("HairEyeColor")
df <- as.data.frame(HairEyeColor)
head(df)
```

```
##     Hair   Eye  Sex Freq
## 1 Black Brown Male   32
## 2 Brown Brown Male   53
## 3   Red Brown Male   10
## 4 Blond Brown Male    3
## 5 Black  Blue Male   11
## 6 Brown  Blue Male   50
```

- Create the bar graph:
    - Hair color on x-axis
    - Change bar fill by Eye color
    - Split the graph into multiple panel by Sex

```
ggplot(df, aes(x = Hair, y = Freq))+
  geom_bar(
    aes(fill = Eye), stat = "identity", color = "white",
    position = position_dodge(0.9)
    )+
  facet_wrap(~Sex) +
  fill_palette("jco")
```

6.4   Balloon plot

Balloon plot is an alternative to bar plot for visualizing a large categorical data. We'll use the function `ggballoonplot()` [in ggpubr], which draws a graphical matrix of a contingency table, where each cell contains a dot whose size reflects the relative magnitude of the corresponding component.

Demo data sets: `Housetasks` (a contingency table containing the frequency of execution of 13 house tasks in the couple.)

```
housetasks <- read.delim(
  system.file("demo-data/housetasks.txt", package = "ggpubr"),
  row.names = 1
  )
head(housetasks, 4)
```

```
##             Wife Alternating Husband Jointly
## Laundry      156          14       2       4
## Main_meal    124          20       5       4
## Dinner        77          11       7      13
## Breakfeast    82          36      15       7
```

- Create a simple balloon plot of a contingency table. Change the fill color by the values in the cells.

```
ggballoonplot(housetasks, fill = "value")+
  scale_fill_viridis_c(option = "C")
```

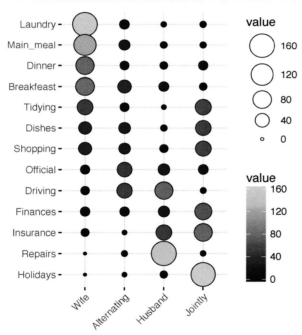

- Visualize a grouped frequency table. Demo data set: `HairEyeColor`. Create a multi-panel plot by Sex

```
df <- as.data.frame(HairEyeColor)
ggballoonplot(df, x = "Hair", y = "Eye", size = "Freq",
              fill = "Freq", facet.by = "Sex",
              ggtheme = theme_bw()) +
  scale_fill_viridis_c(option = "C")
```

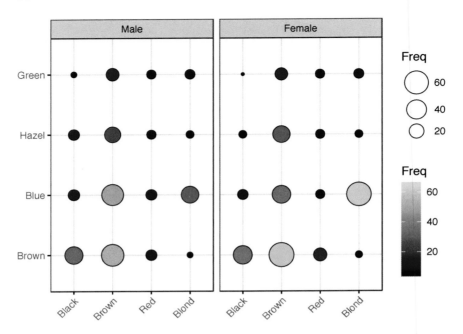

6.5   Mosaic plot

A mosaic plot is basically an area-proportional visualization of observed frequencies, composed of tiles (corresponding to the cells) created by recursive vertical and horizontal splits of a rectangle. The area of each tile is proportional to the corresponding cell entry, given the dimensions of previous splits.

Mosaic graph can be created using either the function `mosaicplot()` [in graphics] or the function `mosaic()` [in vcd package]. Read more at: Visualizing Multi-way Contingency Tables with vcd[2].

Example of mosaic plot:

```
library(vcd)
mosaic(HairEyeColor, shade = TRUE, legend = TRUE)
```

---

[2]https://cran.r-project.org/web/packages/vcd/vignettes/strucplot.pdf

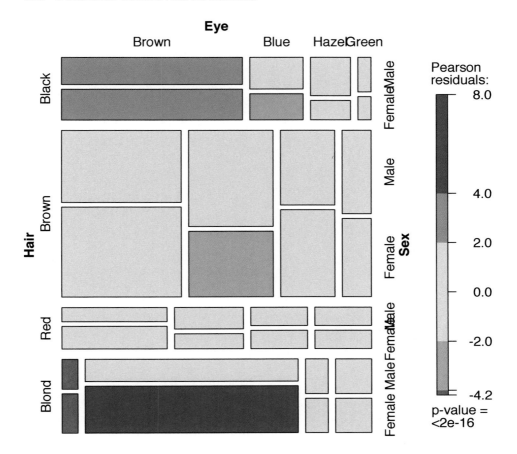

6.6 Correspondence analysis

Correspondence analysis can be used to summarize and visualize the information contained in a large contingency table formed by two categorical variables.

Required package: FactoMineR for the analysis and factoextra for the visualization

```
library(FactoMineR)
library(factoextra)
res.ca <- CA(housetasks, graph = FALSE)
fviz_ca_biplot(res.ca, repel = TRUE)
```

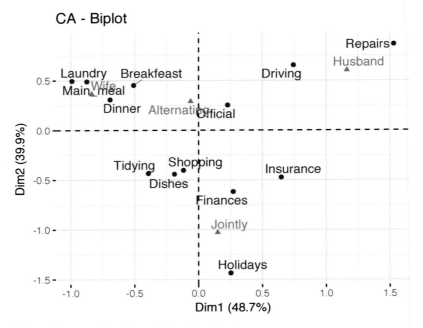

From the graphic above, it's clear that:

- Housetasks such as dinner, breakfeast, laundry are done more often by the wife
- Driving and repairs are done more frequently by the husband

Read more at: Correspondence analysis in R[3]

---

[3]https://goo.gl/7CnpXq

Chapter 7

Plot Time Series Data

7.1 Introduction

In this chapter, we start by describing how to plot simple and multiple time series data using the function `geom_line()`. Next, we show how to set date axis limits and add trend smoothed line to a time series graphs. Finally, we introduce some extensions to the ggplot2 package for easily handling time series objects.

7.2 Basic ggplot of time series

- Plot types: line plot with dates on x-axis
- Demo data set: `economics` [ggplot2] time series data sets are used.

In this section we'll plot the variables `psavert` (personal savings rate) and `uempmed` (number of unemployed in thousands) by `date` (x-axis).

- Load required packages and set the default theme:

```
library(ggplot2)
theme_set(theme_minimal())
# Demo dataset
head(economics)
```

```
## # A tibble: 6 x 6
##         date   pce    pop psavert uempmed unemploy
##       <date> <dbl>  <int>   <dbl>   <dbl>    <int>
## 1 1967-07-01   507 198712    12.5     4.5     2944
## 2 1967-08-01   510 198911    12.5     4.7     2945
## 3 1967-09-01   516 199113    11.7     4.6     2958
## 4 1967-10-01   513 199311    12.5     4.9     3143
## 5 1967-11-01   518 199498    12.5     4.7     3066
## 6 1967-12-01   526 199657    12.1     4.8     3018
```

- Create basic line plots

```
# Basic line plot
ggplot(data = economics, aes(x = date, y = pop))+
  geom_line(color = "#00AFBB", size = 2)

# Plot a subset of the data
ss <- subset(economics, date > as.Date("2006-1-1"))
ggplot(data = ss, aes(x = date, y = pop)) +
  geom_line(color = "#FC4E07", size = 2)
```

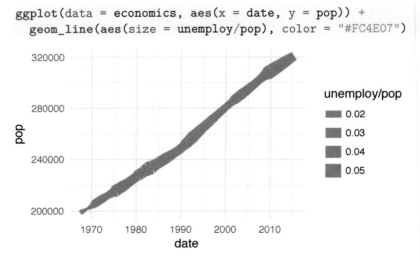

- Control line size by the value of a continuous variable:

```
ggplot(data = economics, aes(x = date, y = pop)) +
  geom_line(aes(size = unemploy/pop), color = "#FC4E07")
```

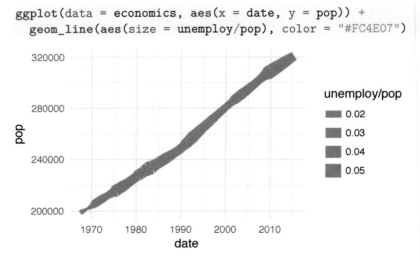

7.3   Plot multiple time series data

Here, we'll plot the variables **psavert** and **uempmed** by dates. You should first reshape the data using the `tidyr` package: - Collapse **psavert** and **uempmed** values in the same column (new column). R function: `gather()` `[tidyr]` - Create a grouping variable that with levels = **psavert** and **uempmed**

```
library(tidyr)
library(dplyr)
```

```
df <- economics %>%
  select(date, psavert, uempmed) %>%
  gather(key = "variable", value = "value", -date)
head(df, 3)
```

```
## # A tibble: 3 x 3
##        date variable value
##      <date>    <chr> <dbl>
## 1 1967-07-01  psavert  12.5
## 2 1967-08-01  psavert  12.5
## 3 1967-09-01  psavert  11.7
```

```
# Multiple line plot
ggplot(df, aes(x = date, y = value)) +
  geom_line(aes(color = variable), size = 1) +
  scale_color_manual(values = c("#00AFBB", "#E7B800")) +
  theme_minimal()
```

```
# Area plot
ggplot(df, aes(x = date, y = value)) +
  geom_area(aes(color = variable, fill = variable),
            alpha = 0.5, position = position_dodge(0.8)) +
  scale_color_manual(values = c("#00AFBB", "#E7B800")) +
  scale_fill_manual(values = c("#00AFBB", "#E7B800"))
```

7.4   Set date axis limits

Key R function: `scale_x_date()`

```
# Base plot with date axis
p <- ggplot(data = economics, aes(x = date, y = psavert)) +
    geom_line(color = "#00AFBB", size = 1)
p

# Set axis limits c(min, max)
min <- as.Date("2002-1-1")
max <- NA
p + scale_x_date(limits = c(min, max))
```

7.5   Format date axis labels

Key function: `scale_x_date()`.

To format date axis labels, you can use different combinations of days, weeks, months and years:

- Weekday name: use `%a` and `%A` for abbreviated and full weekday name, respectively
- Month name: use `%b` and `%B` for abbreviated and full month name, respectively
- `%d`: day of the month as decimal number
- `%Y`: Year with century.
- See more options in the documentation of the function `?strptime`

```
# Format : month/year
p + scale_x_date(date_labels = "%b/%Y")
```

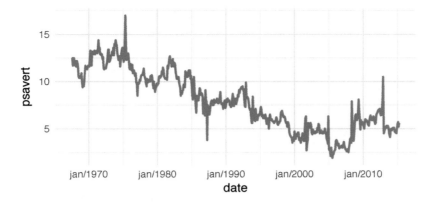

7.6 Add trend smoothed line

Key function: `stat_smooth()`

```
p + stat_smooth(
  color = "#FC4E07", fill = "#FC4E07",
  method = "loess"
  )
```

7.7 ggplot2 extensions for ts objects

The `ggfortify` package is an extension to ggplot2 that makes it easy to plot time series objects (Horikoshi and Tang, 2017). It can handle the output of many time series packages, including: zoo::zooreg(), xts::xts(), timeSeries::timSeries(), tseries::irts(), forecast::forecast(), vars:vars().

Another interesting package is the `ggpmisc` package (Aphalo, 2017), which provides two useful methods for time series object:

- `stat_peaks()` finds at which x positions local y maxima are located, and
- `stat_valleys()` finds at which x positions local y minima are located.

Here, we'll show how to easily:

- Visualize a time series object, using the data set `AirPassengers` (monthly airline passenger numbers 1949-1960).
- Identify shifts in mean and/or variance in a time series using the `changepoint` package.
- Detect jumps in a data using the `strucchange` package and the data set `Nile` (Measurements of the annual flow of the river Nile at Aswan).
- Detect peaks and valleys using the `ggpmisc` package and the data set `lynx` (Annual Canadian Lynx trappings 1821–1934).

First, install required R packages:

```r
install.packages(
  c("ggfortify", "changepoint",
    "strucchange", "ggpmisc")
)
```

Then use the `autoplot.ts()` function to visualize time series objects, as follow:

```r
library(ggfortify)
library(magrittr) # for piping %>%

# Plot ts objects
autoplot(AirPassengers)

# Identify change points in mean and variance
AirPassengers %>%
  changepoint:: cpt.meanvar() %>%  # Identify change points
  autoplot()

# Detect jump in a data
strucchange::breakpoints(Nile ~ 1) %>%
  autoplot()
```

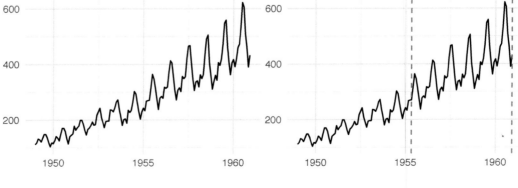

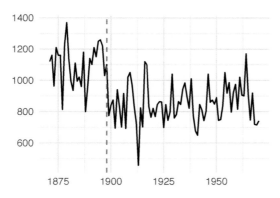

Detect peaks and valleys:

```
library(ggpmisc)
ggplot(lynx, as.numeric = FALSE) + geom_line() +
  stat_peaks(colour = "red") +
  stat_peaks(geom = "text", colour = "red",
             vjust = -0.5, x.label.fmt = "%Y") +
  stat_valleys(colour = "blue") +
  stat_valleys(geom = "text", colour = "blue", angle = 45,
               vjust = 1.5, hjust = 1,  x.label.fmt = "%Y")+
  ylim(-500, 7300)
```

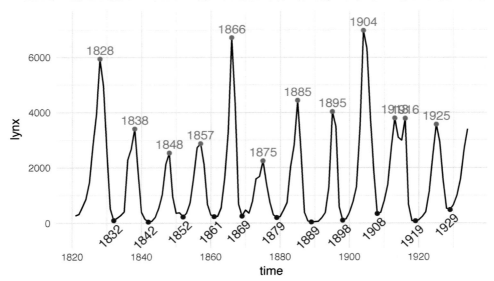

Chapter 8

Facets: Multi-Panels GGPlot

8.1 Introduction

This chapter describes how to create a multi-panel ggplots or facets. Facets divide a ggplot into subplots based on the values of one or more categorical variables. There are two main functions for faceting: `facet_grid()` and `facet_wrap()`

8.2 Prerequisites

Load required packages and set the theme function `theme_light()` [ggplot2] as the default theme:

```
library(ggplot2)
theme_set(
  theme_light() + theme(legend.position = "top")
  )
```

Create a box plot filled by groups:

```
# Load data and convert dose to a factor variable
data("ToothGrowth")
ToothGrowth$dose <- as.factor(ToothGrowth$dose)
# Box plot
p <- ggplot(ToothGrowth, aes(x = dose, y = len)) +
  geom_boxplot(aes(fill = supp), position = position_dodge(0.9)) +
  scale_fill_manual(values = c("#00AFBB", "#E7B800"))
p
```

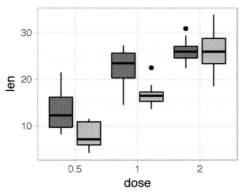

8.3 Split the plot into a matrix of panels

The following functions can be used for facets:

- p + **facet_grid**(supp ~ .): Facet in vertical direction based on the levels of *supp* variable.

- p + **facet_grid**(. ~ supp): Facet in horizontal direction based on the levels of *supp* variable.

- p + **facet_grid**(dose ~ supp): Facet in horizontal and vertical directions based on two variables: *dose* and *supp*.
- p + **facet_wrap**(~ fl): Place facet side by side into a rectangular layout

1. **Facet with one discrete variable**: Split by the levels of the group "supp"

```
# Split in vertical direction
p + facet_grid(supp ~ .)

# Split in horizontal direction
p + facet_grid(. ~ supp)
```

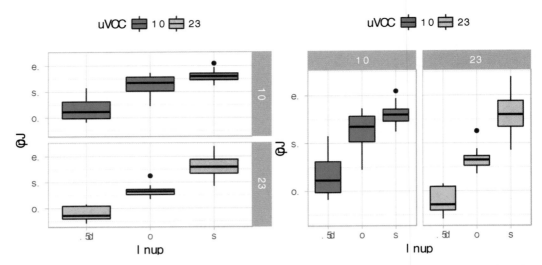

2. **Facet with two discrete variables**: Split by the levels of the groups "dose" and
   "supp"

```
# Facet by two variables: dose and supp.
# Rows are dose and columns are supp
p + facet_grid(dose ~ supp)
```

```
# Facet by two variables: reverse the order of the 2 variables
# Rows are supp and columns are dose
p + facet_grid(supp ~ dose)
```

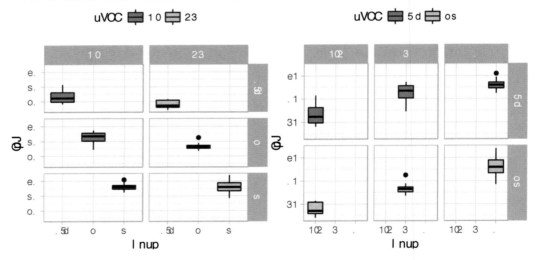

Note that, you can use the argument `margins` to add additional facets which contain all
the data for each of the possible values of the faceting variables

```
p + facet_grid(dose ~ supp, margins=TRUE)
```

3. **Facet scales**

By default, all the panels have the same scales (`scales="fixed"`). They can be made independent, by setting scales to `free`, `free_x`, or `free_y`.

```
p + facet_grid(dose ~ supp, scales='free')
```

4. **Facet labels**: The argument `labeller` can be used to control the labels of the panels.

```
p + facet_grid(dose ~ supp, labeller=label_both)
```

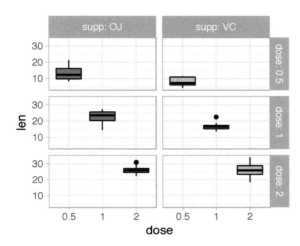

The appearance of facet labels can be modified as follow :

```
# Change facet text font. Possible values for the font style:
#'plain', 'italic', 'bold', 'bold.italic'.
p + facet_grid(dose ~ supp)+
   theme(strip.text.x = element_text(size=12, color="red",
                                     face="bold.italic"),
         strip.text.y = element_text(size=12, color="red",
                                     face="bold.italic"))


# Change the apperance of the rectangle around facet label
p + facet_grid(dose ~ supp)+
 theme(strip.background = element_rect(color="black", fill="#FC4E07",
                                       size=1.5, linetype="solid"))
```

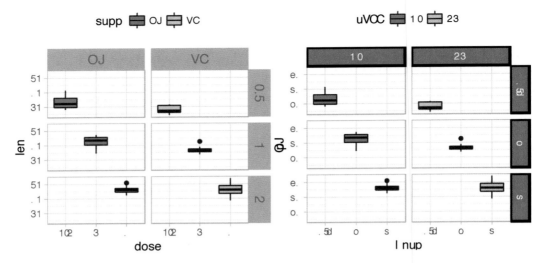

5. **facet_wrap**: Facets can be placed side by side using the function `facet_wrap()` as follow :

```
p + facet_wrap(~ dose)
```

```
p + facet_wrap(~ dose, ncol=2)
```

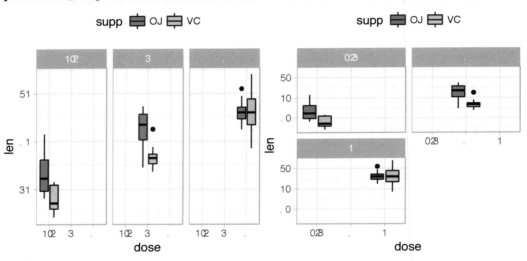

8.4   See also

- Create and Customize Multi-panel ggplots: Easy Guide to Facet. `https://goo.gl/eRKHV7`

Chapter 9

Arrange Multiple GGPlot on One Page

9.1 Introduction

This chapter describes, step by step, how to combine **multiple ggplot** on one page, as well as, over multiple pages, using helper functions available in the *ggpubr* R package. We'll also describe how to export the arranged plots to a file.

9.2 Prerequisites

Load required packages and set the theme function `theme_pubr()` [in ggpubr] as the default theme:

```
library(ggplot2)
library(ggpubr)
theme_set(theme_pubr())
```

9.3 Arrange on one page

- **Create some basic plots** as follow:

```
# 0. Define custom color palette and prepare the data
my3cols <- c("#E7B800", "#2E9FDF", "#FC4E07")
ToothGrowth$dose <- as.factor(ToothGrowth$dose)

# 1. Create a box plot (bp)
p <- ggplot(ToothGrowth, aes(x = dose, y = len))
bxp <- p + geom_boxplot(aes(color = dose)) +
  scale_color_manual(values = my3cols)
```

```
# 2. Create a dot plot (dp)
dp <- p + geom_dotplot(aes(color = dose, fill = dose),
                       binaxis='y', stackdir='center') +
  scale_color_manual(values = my3cols) +
  scale_fill_manual(values = my3cols)

# 3. Create a line plot
lp <- ggplot(economics, aes(x = date, y = psavert)) +
  geom_line(color = "#E46726")
```

- **Combine multiple ggplot on one page**. Use the function `ggarrange()` [ggpubr package], a wrapper around the function `plot_grid()` [cowplot package]. Compared to plot_grid(), ggarange() can arrange multiple ggplots over multiple pages.

```
figure <- ggarrange(bxp, dp, lp,
                    labels = c("A", "B", "C"),
                    ncol = 2, nrow = 2)
figure
```

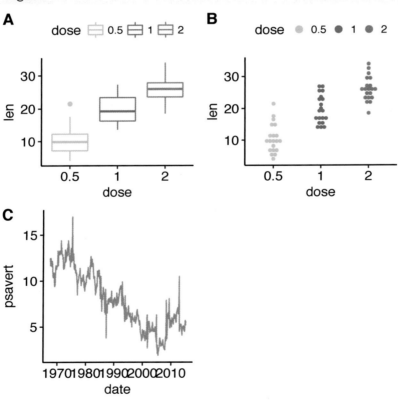

9.4   Annotate the arranged figure

Key R function: `annotate_figure()` [in ggpubr].

```
annotate_figure(
  figure,
  top = text_grob("Visualizing len",
                  color = "red", face = "bold", size = 14),
  bottom = text_grob("Data source: \n ToothGrowth", color = "blue",
                     hjust = 1, x = 1, face = "italic", size = 10),
  left = text_grob("Fig arranged using ggpubr",
                  color = "green", rot = 90),
  right = "I'm done, thanks :-)!",
  fig.lab = "Figure 1", fig.lab.face = "bold"
  )
```

9.5 Change column and row span of a plot

We'll use nested **ggarrange()** functions to change column/row span of plots. For example, using the R code below:

- the line plot (lp) will live in the first row and spans over two columns
- the box plot (bxp) and the dot plot (dp) will be first arranged and will live in the second row with two different columns

```
ggarrange(
  lp,                     # First row with line plot
  # Second row with box and dot plots
  ggarrange(bxp, dp, ncol = 2, labels = c("B", "C")),
  nrow = 2,
  labels = "A"            # Label of the line plot
  )
```

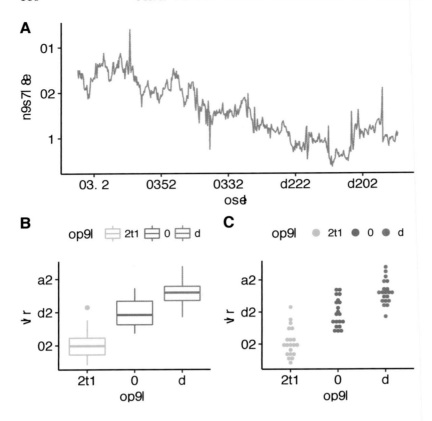

9.6   Use shared legend for combined ggplots

To place a common unique legend in the margin of the arranged plots, the function `ggarrange()` [in ggpubr] can be used with the following arguments:

- `common.legend = TRUE`: place a common legend in a margin
- `legend`: specify the legend position. Allowed values include one of c("top", "bottom", "left", "right")

```
ggarrange(
  bxp, dp, labels = c("A", "B"),
  common.legend = TRUE, legend = "bottom"
  )
```

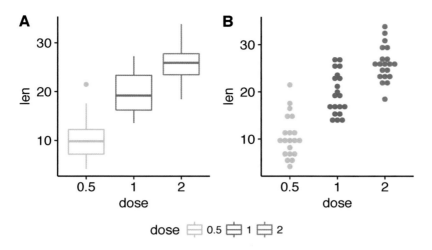

9.7 Mix table, text and ggplot2 graphs

In this section, we'll show how to plot a table and text alongside a chart. The iris data set will be used.

We start by creating the following plots:

1. a **density plot** of the variable "Sepal.Length". R function: **ggdensity**() [in ggpubr]
2. a plot of the **summary table** containing the descriptive statistics (mean, sd, ...) of Sepal.Length.
    - R function for computing descriptive statistics: **desc_statby**() [in ggpubr].
    - R function to draw a textual table: **ggtexttable**() [in ggpubr].
3. a plot of a text **paragraph**. R function: **ggparagraph**() [in ggpubr].

We finish by arranging/combining the three plots using the function **ggarrange**() [in ggpubr]

```
# Density plot of "Sepal.Length"
#::::::::::::::::::::::::::::::::::::::
density.p <- ggdensity(iris, x = "Sepal.Length",
                       fill = "Species", palette = "jco")


# Draw the summary table of Sepal.Length
#::::::::::::::::::::::::::::::::::::::
# Compute descriptive statistics by groups
stable <- desc_statby(iris, measure.var = "Sepal.Length",
                      grps = "Species")
stable <- stable[, c("Species", "length", "mean", "sd")]
# Summary table plot, medium orange theme
stable.p <- ggtexttable(stable, rows = NULL,
                        theme = ttheme("mOrange"))


# Draw text
```

```
#::::::::::::::::::::::::::::::::::::::::::
text <- paste("iris data set gives the measurements in cm",
              "of the variables sepal length and width",
              "and petal length and width, respectively,",
              "for 50 flowers from each of 3 species of iris.",
              "The species are Iris setosa, versicolor, and virginica.",
              sep = " ")
text.p <- ggparagraph(text = text, face = "italic", size = 11, color = "black")

# Arrange the plots on the same page
ggarrange(density.p, stable.p, text.p,
          ncol = 1, nrow = 3,
          heights = c(1, 0.5, 0.3))
```

Species	length	mean	sd
setosa	50	5.01	0.352
versicolor	50	5.94	0.516
virginica	50	6.59	0.636

iris data set gives the measurements in cm of the variables sepal length and width and petal length and width, respectively, for 50 flowers from each of 3 species of iris. The species are Iris setosa, versicolor, and virginica.

9.8 Arrange over multiple pages

If you have a long list of ggplots, say n = 20 plots, you may want to arrange the plots and to place them on multiple pages. With 4 plots per page, you need 5 pages to hold the 20 plots.

The function **ggarrange()** [ggpubr] provides a convenient solution to arrange multiple ggplots over multiple pages. After specifying the arguments `nrow` and `ncol`, ggarrange()' computes automatically the number of pages required to hold the list of the plots. It returns a list of arranged ggplots.

For example the following R code,

```
multi.page <- ggarrange(bxp, dp, lp, bxp,
                        nrow = 1, ncol = 2)
```

returns a list of two pages with two plots per page. You can visualize each page as follow:

```
multi.page[[1]] # Visualize page 1
multi.page[[2]] # Visualize page 2
```

You can also export the arranged plots to a pdf file using the function `ggexport()` [ggpubr]:

```
ggexport(multi.page, filename = "multi.page.ggplot2.pdf")
```

See the PDF file: Multi.page.ggplot2[1]

9.9 Export the arranged plots

R function: `ggexport()` [in ggpubr].

- Export the arranged figure to a pdf, eps or png file (one figure per page).

```
ggexport(figure, filename = "figure1.pdf")
```

- It's also possible to arrange the plots (2 plot per page) when exporting them.

Export individual plots to a pdf file (one plot per page):

```
ggexport(bxp, dp, lp, bxp, filename = "test.pdf")
```

Arrange and export. Specify nrow and ncol to display multiple plots on the same page:

```
ggexport(bxp, dp, lp, bxp, filename = "test.pdf",
         nrow = 2, ncol = 1)
```

9.10 See also

- ggplot2 - Easy Way to Mix Multiple Graphs on The Same Page. `https://goo.gl/WrieY4`

---

[1] `//www.slideshare.net/kassambara/multipageggplot2`

Chapter 10

Customize GGPlot

In this chapter, we'll show how to change the global appearance of a ggplot.

10.1 Prerequisites

1. Load packages and set the default theme:

```
library(ggplot2)
library(ggpubr)
theme_set(
  theme_pubr() +
    theme(legend.position = "right")
)
```

2. Create a box plot (bxp) and a scatter plot (sp) that we'll customize in the next section:

- Box plot using the `ToothGrowth` dataset:

```
# Convert the variable dose from numeric to factor variable
ToothGrowth$dose <- as.factor(ToothGrowth$dose)
bxp <- ggplot(ToothGrowth, aes(x=dose, y=len)) +
  geom_boxplot(aes(color = dose)) +
  scale_color_manual(values = c("#00AFBB", "#E7B800", "#FC4E07"))
```

- Scatter plot using the `cars` dataset

```
sp <- ggplot(cars, aes(x = speed, y = dist)) +
  geom_point()
```

10.2 Titles and axis labels

Key function: `labs()`. Used to change the main title, the subtitle, the axis labels and captions.

1. **Add a title, subtitle, caption and change axis labels**

```
bxp <- bxp + labs(title = "Effect of Vitamin C on Tooth Growth",
              subtitle = "Plot of length by dose",
              caption = "Data source: ToothGrowth",
              x = "Dose (mg)", y = "Teeth length")
bxp
```

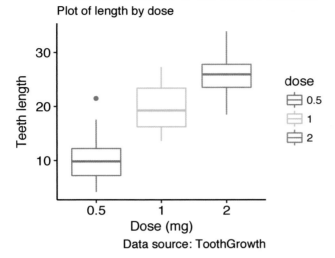

2. **Change the appearance of titles**

- Key functions: `theme()` and `element_text()`:

```
theme(
  plot.title = element_text(),
  plot.subtitle.title = element_text(),
  plot.caption = element_text()
)
```

- Arguments of the function `element_text()` include:
    - `color, size, face, family`: to change the text font color, size, face ("plain", "italic", "bold", "bold.italic") and family.
    - `lineheight`: change space between two lines of text elements. Number between 0 and 1. Useful for multi-line plot titles.
    - `hjust` and `vjust`: number in [0, 1], for horizontal and vertical adjustement of titles, respectively.
        * `hjust = 0.5`: Center the plot titles.
        * `hjust = 1`: Place the plot title on the right
        * `hjust = 0`: Place the plot title on the left
- Examples of R code:
    - Center main title and subtitle (`hjust = 0.5`)
    - Change color, size and face

```
bxp + theme(
  plot.title = element_text(color = "red", size = 12,
                            face = "bold", hjust = 0.5),
  plot.subtitle = element_text(color = "blue", hjust = 0.5),
  plot.caption = element_text(color = "green", face = "italic")
)
```

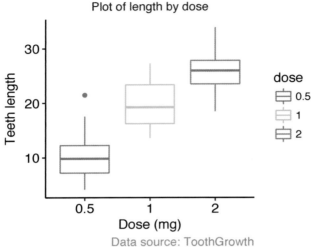

3. **Case of long titles**. If the title is too long, you can split it into multiple lines using \n. In this case you can adjust the space between text lines by specifying the argument `lineheight` in the theme function `element_text()`:

```
bxp + labs(title = "Effect of Vitamin C on Tooth Growth \n in Guinea Pigs")+
  theme(plot.title = element_text(lineheight = 0.9))
```

10.3   Axes: Limits, Ticks and Log

10.3.1   Axis limits and scales

3 Key functions to set the axis limits and scales:

1. Without clipping (preferred). Cartesian coordinates. The Cartesian coordinate system is the most common type of coordinate system. It will zoom the plot, without clipping the data.

```
sp + coord_cartesian(xlim = c(5, 20), ylim = (0, 50))
```

2. With clipping the data (removes unseen data points). Observations not in this range will be dropped completely and not passed to any other layers.

```
# Use this
sp + scale_x_continuous(limits = c(5, 20)) +
```

```
scale_y_continuous(limits = c(0, 50))

# Or this shothand functions
sp + xlim(5, 20) + ylim(0, 50)
```

> Note that, `scale_x_continuous()` and `scale_y_continuous()` remove all data points outside the given range and, the `coord_cartesian()` function only adjusts the visible area.
>
> In most cases you would not see the difference, but if you fit anything to the data the functions `scale_x_continuous()` / `scale_y_continuous()` would probably change the fitted values.

3. Expand the plot limits to ensure that a given value is included in all panels or all plots.

```
# set the intercept of x and y axes at (0,0)
sp + expand_limits(x = 0, y = 0)

# Expand plot limits
sp + expand_limits(x = c(5, 50), y = c(0, 150))
```

Examples of R code:

```
# Default plot
print(sp)

# Change axis limits using coord_cartesian()
sp + coord_cartesian(xlim =c(5, 20), ylim = c(0, 50))

# set the intercept of x and y axis at (0,0)
sp + expand_limits(x = 0, y = 0)
```

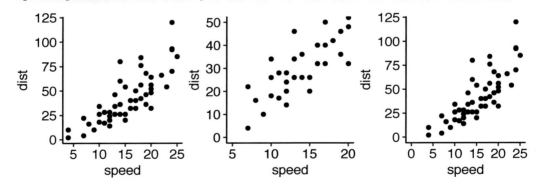

10:3.2   Log scale

Key functions to set a logarithmic axis scale:

1. Scale functions. Allowed value for the argument trans: `log2` and `log10`.

```
sp + scale_x_continuous(trans = "log2")

sp + scale_y_continuous(trans = "log2")
```

2. Transformed cartesian coordinate system. Possible values for x and y are "log2", "log10", "sqrt", ...

```
sp + coord_trans(x = "log2", y = "log2")
```

3. Display log scale ticks. Make sens only for log10 scale:

```
sp + scale_y_log10() + annotation_logticks()
```

> Note that, the scale functions transform the data. If you fit anything to the data it would probably change the fitted values.
>
> An alternative is to use the function *coord_trans()*, which occurs after statistical transformation and will affect only the visual appearance of geoms.

Example of R code

```
# Set axis into log2 scale
# Possible values for trans : 'log2', 'log10','sqrt'
sp + scale_x_continuous(trans = 'log2') +
  scale_y_continuous(trans = 'log2')

# Format y axis tick mark labels to show exponents
require(scales)
sp + scale_y_continuous(
  trans = log2_trans(),
  breaks = trans_breaks("log2", function(x) 2^x),
  labels = trans_format("log2", math_format(2^.x))
  )
```

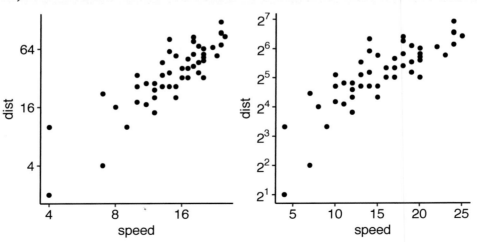

10.3.3 Axis Ticks: Set and Rotate Text Labels

Start by creating a box plot:

```
bxp <- ggplot(ToothGrowth, aes(x=dose, y=len)) +
  geom_boxplot(aes(color = dose)) +
  scale_color_manual(values = c("#00AFBB", "#E7B800", "#FC4E07"))+
  theme(legend.position = "none")
```

1. **Change the style and the orientation angle of axis tick labels.** For a vertical rotation of x axis labels use `angle = 90`.

```
# Rotate x and y axis text by 45 degree
# face can be "plain", "italic", "bold" or "bold.italic"
bxp + theme(axis.text.x = element_text(face = "bold", color = "#993333",
                         size = 12, angle = 45),
          axis.text.y = element_text(face = "bold", color = "blue",
                         size = 12, angle = 45))
```

```
# Remove axis ticks and tick mark labels
bxp + theme(
  axis.text.x = element_blank(), # Remove x axis tick labels
  axis.text.y = element_blank(), # Remove y axis tick labels
  axis.ticks = element_blank()    # Remove ticks
  )
```

To adjust the postion of the axis text, you can specify the argument `hjust` and `vjust`, which values should be comprised between 0 and 1.

2. **Change axis lines:**
    - Remove the y-axis line
    - Change the color, the size and the line type of the x-axis line:

```
bxp + theme(
  axis.line.y = element_blank(),
  axis.line = element_line(
    color = "gray", size = 1, linetype = "solid"
    )
  )
```

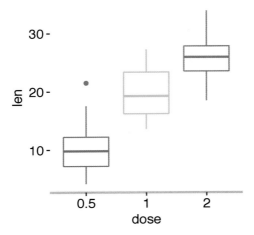

3. **Customize discrete axis**.   Use the function `scale_x_discrete()` or `scale_y_discrete()` depending on the axis you want to change.

Here, we'll customize the x-axis of the box plot:

```
# Change x axis label and the order of items
bxp + scale_x_discrete(name ="Dose (mg)",
                       limits = c("2","1","0.5"))


# Rename / Change tick mark labels
bxp + scale_x_discrete(breaks = c("0.5","1","2"),
       labels = c("D0.5", "D1", "D2"))


# Choose which items to display
bxp + scale_x_discrete(limits = c("0.5", "2"))
```

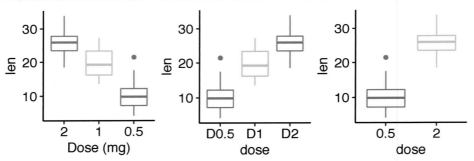

4. **Customize continuous axis**. Change axis ticks interval.

```
# Default scatter plot
sp <- ggplot(cars, aes(x = speed, y = dist)) +
  geom_point()
sp


# Break y axis by a specified value
# a tick mark is shown on every 50
sp + scale_y_continuous(breaks=seq(0, 150, 50))
```

```
# Tick marks can be spaced randomly
sp + scale_y_continuous(breaks=c(0, 50, 65, 75, 150))
```

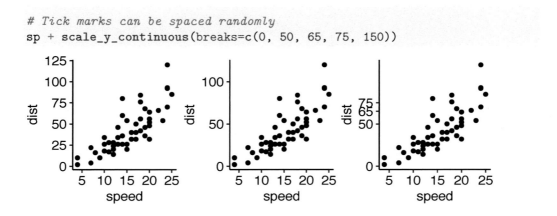

10.4 Legends: Title, Position and Appearance

Start by creating a box plot using the `ToothGrowth` data set. Change the box plot fill color according to the grouping variable `dose`.

```
library(ggplot2)
ToothGrowth$dose <- as.factor(ToothGrowth$dose)
bxp <- ggplot(ToothGrowth, aes(x = dose, y = len))+
  geom_boxplot(aes(fill = dose)) +
  scale_fill_manual(values = c("#00AFBB", "#E7B800", "#FC4E07"))
```

10.4.1 Change legend title and position

1. **Legend title**. Use `labs()` to changes the legend title for a given aesthetics (fill, color, size, shape, . . .). For example:

   - Use `p + labs(fill = "dose")` for geom_boxplot(aes(fill = dose))
   - Use `p + labs(color = "dose")` for geom_boxplot(aes(color = dose))
   - and so on for linetype, shape, etc

2. **Legend position**. The default legend position is "right". Use the function `theme()` with the argument `legend.position` to specify the legend position.

Allowed values for the legend position include: "left", "top", "right", "bottom", "none".

Legend loction can be also a numeric vector c(x,y), where x and y are the coordinates of the legend box. Their values should be between 0 and 1. c(0,0) corresponds to the "bottom left" and c(1,1) corresponds to the "top right" position. This makes it possible to place the legend inside the plot.

Examples:

```
# Default plot
bxp
```

```
# Change legend title and position
bxp +
  labs(fill = "Dose (mg)") +
  theme(legend.position = "top")
```

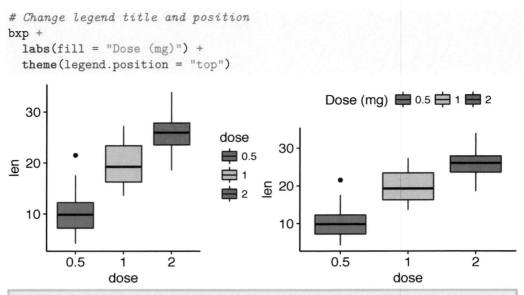

To remove legend, use p + theme(legend.position = "none").

10.4.2   Change the appearance of legends

- Change legend text color and size
- Change the legend box background color

```
# Change the appearance of legend title and text labels
bxp + theme(
  legend.title = element_text(color = "blue", size = 10),
  legend.text = element_text(color = "red")
  )
```

```
# Change legend background color, key size and width
bxp + theme(
  # Change legend background color
  legend.background = element_rect(fill = "darkgray"),
  legend.key = element_rect(fill = "lightblue", color = NA),
  # Change legend key size and key width
  legend.key.size = unit(1.5, "cm"),
  legend.key.width = unit(0.5,"cm")
  )
```

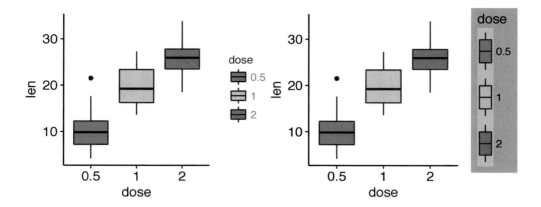

10.4.3 Rename legend labels and change the order of items

```
# Change the order of legend items
bxp + scale_x_discrete(limits=c("2", "0.5", "1"))

# Edit legend title and labels for the fill aesthetics
bxp + scale_fill_manual(
  values = c("#00AFBB", "#E7B800", "#FC4E07"),
  name = "Dose",
  breaks = c("0.5", "1", "2"),
  labels = c("D0.5", "D1", "D2")
  )
```

Other manual scales to set legends for a given aesthetic:

```
# Color of lines and points
scale_color_manual(name, labels, limits, breaks)
# For linetypes
scale_linetype_manual(name, labels, limits, breaks)
# For point shapes
scale_shape_manual(name, labels, limits, breaks)
```

```
# For point size
scale_size_manual(name, labels, limits, breaks)
# Opacity/transparency
scale_alpha_manual(name, labels, limits, breaks)
```

10.5   Themes gallery

Start by creating a simple box plot:

```
bxp <- ggplot(ToothGrowth, aes(x = factor(dose), y = len)) +
  geom_boxplot()
```

10.5.1   Use themes in ggplot2 package

Several simple functions are available in ggplot2 package to set easily a ggplot theme.
These include:

- `theme_gray()`: Gray background color and white grid lines. Put the data forward
  to make comparisons easy.
- `theme_bw()`: White background and gray grid lines. May work better for presentations displayed with a projector.
- `theme_linedraw()`: A theme with black lines of various widths on white backgrounds, reminiscent of a line drawings.
- `theme_light()`: A theme similar to `theme_linedraw()` but with light grey lines
  and axes, to direct more attention towards the data.

```
bxp + theme_gray(base_size = 14)

bxp + theme_bw()

bxp + theme_linedraw()

bxp + theme_light()
```

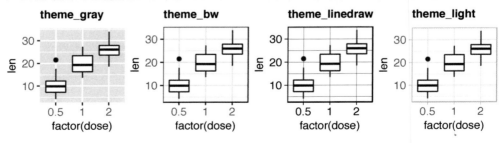

- `theme_dark()`: Same as theme_light but with a dark background. Useful to make
  thin coloured lines pop out.
- `theme_minimal()`: A minimal theme with no background annotations
- `theme_classic()`: A classic theme, with x and y axis lines and no gridlines.

- `theme_void()`: a completely empty theme, useful for plots with non-standard coordinates or for drawings.

```
bxp + theme_dark()

bxp + theme_minimal()

bxp + theme_classic()

bxp + theme_void()
```

> Note that, additional themes are availbale in the ggthemes R package[a].
> _____
> [a]https://cran.r-project.org/web/packages/ggthemes/vignettes/ggthemes.html

10.6 Background color and grid lines

- Create a simple box plot:

```
p <- ggplot(ToothGrowth, aes(factor(dose), len)) +
  geom_boxplot()
```

- Change the panel background (1) and the plot background (2) colors:

```
# 1. Change plot panel background color to lightblue
# and the color of major/grid lines to white
p + theme(
  panel.background = element_rect(fill = "#BFD5E3", colour = "#6D9EC1",
                                  size = 2, linetype = "solid"),
  panel.grid.major = element_line(size = 0.5, linetype = 'solid',
                                  colour = "white"),
  panel.grid.minor = element_line(size = 0.25, linetype = 'solid',
                                  colour = "white")
)

# 2. Change the plot background color (not the panel)
p + theme(plot.background = element_rect(fill = "#BFD5E3"))
```

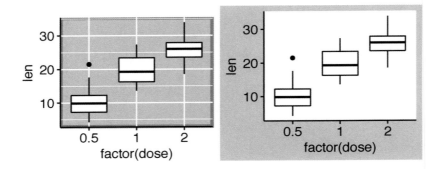

10.7   Add background image to ggplot2 graphs

1. **Import the background image**. Use either the function readJPEG() [in *jpeg* package] or the function 'readPNG()[in *png* package] depending on the format of the background image.

2. **Combine a ggplot with the background image**. R function: background_image() [in ggpubr].

```
# Import the image
img.file <- system.file(file.path("images", "background-image.png"),
                          package = "ggpubr")
img <- png::readPNG(img.file)

# Combine with ggplot
library(ggpubr)
ggplot(iris, aes(Species, Sepal.Length))+
  background_image(img)+
  geom_boxplot(aes(fill = Species), color = "white", alpha = 0.5)+
  fill_palette("jco")
```

10.8 Colors

A color can be specified either by name (e.g.: "red") or by hexadecimal code (e.g. : "#FF1234"). In this section, you will learn how to change ggplot colors by groups and how to set gradient colors.

0. **Set ggplot theme** to `theme_minimal()`:

```
theme_set(
  theme_minimal() +
    theme(legend.position = "top")
  )
```

1. **Initialize ggplots** using the `iris` data set:

```
# Box plot
bp <- ggplot(iris, aes(Species, Sepal.Length))

# Scatter plot
sp <- ggplot(iris, aes(Sepal.Length, Sepal.Width))
```

2. **Specify a single color**. Change the fill color (in box plots) and points color (in scatter plots).

```
# Box plot
bp + geom_boxplot(fill = "#FFDB6D", color = "#C4961A")

# Scatter plot
sp + geom_point(color = "#00AFBB")
```

3. **Change colors by groups**.

You can change colors according to a grouping variable by:

- Mapping the argument `color` to the variable of interest. This will be applied to points, lines and texts

- Mapping the argument `fill` to the variable of interest. This will change the fill color of areas, such as in box plot, bar plot, histogram, density plots, etc.

It's possible to specify manually the color palettes by using the functions:

- `scale_fill_manual()` for box plot, bar plot, violin plot, dot plot, etc
- `scale_color_manual()` or `scale_colour_manual()` for lines and points

```
# Box plot
bp <- bp + geom_boxplot(aes(fill = Species))
bp + scale_fill_manual(values = c("#00AFBB", "#E7B800", "#FC4E07"))

# Scatter plot
sp <- sp + geom_point(aes(color = Species))
sp + scale_color_manual(values = c("#00AFBB", "#E7B800", "#FC4E07"))
```

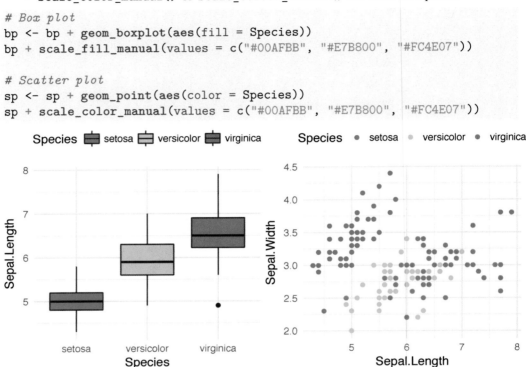

Find below, two color-blind-friendly palettes, one with gray, and one with black (source: http://jfly.iam.u-tokyo.ac.jp/color/).

```
# The palette with grey:
cbp1 <- c("#999999", "#E69F00", "#56B4E9", "#009E73",
          "#F0E442", "#0072B2", "#D55E00", "#CC79A7")

# The palette with black:
cbp2 <- c("#000000", "#E69F00", "#56B4E9", "#009E73",
          "#F0E442", "#0072B2", "#D55E00", "#CC79A7")
```

4. **Use viridis color palettes**. The `viridis` R package provides color palettes to make beautiful plots that are: printer-friendly, perceptually uniform and easy to read by those with colorblindness. Key functions `scale_color_viridis()` and

```
      scale_fill_viridis()
library(viridis)
# Gradient color
ggplot(iris, aes(Sepal.Length, Sepal.Width))+
  geom_point(aes(color = Sepal.Length)) +
  scale_color_viridis(option = "D")

# Discrete color. use the argument discrete = TRUE
ggplot(iris, aes(Sepal.Length, Sepal.Width))+
  geom_point(aes(color = Species)) +
  geom_smooth(aes(color = Species, fill = Species), method = "lm") +
  scale_color_viridis(discrete = TRUE, option = "D")+
  scale_fill_viridis(discrete = TRUE)
```

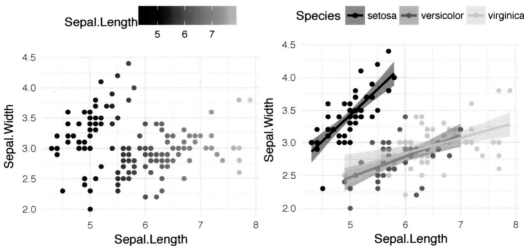

5. **Use RColorBrewer palettes**. Two color scale functions are available in ggplot2 for using the colorbrewer palettes:

- scale_fill_brewer() for box plot, bar plot, violin plot, dot plot, etc
- scale_color_brewer() for lines and points

For example:

```
# Box plot
bp + scale_fill_brewer(palette = "Dark2")

# Scatter plot
sp + scale_color_brewer(palette = "Dark2")
```

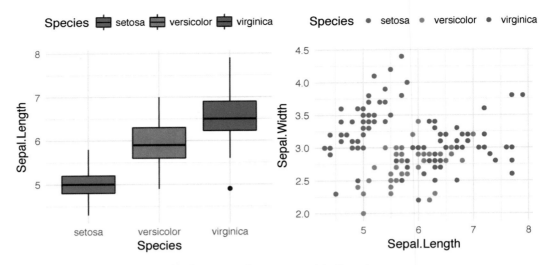

To display colorblind-friendly brewer palettes, use this R code:

```
library(RColorBrewer)
display.brewer.all(colorblindFriendly = TRUE)
```

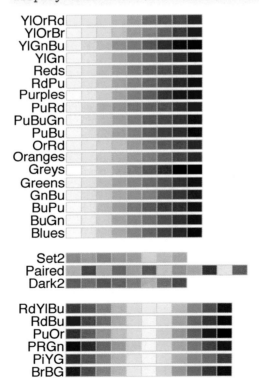

6. **Other discrete color palettes**:
   - **Scientific journal color palettes in the ggsci R package**. Contains a collection of high-quality color palettes inspired by colors used in scientific journals, data visualization libraries, and more. For example:

      – `scale_color_npg()` and `scale_fill_npg()`: Nature Publishing Group
      – `scale_color_aaas()` and `scale_fill_aaas()`: American Association for the Advancement of Science
      – `scale_color_lancet()` and `scale_fill_lancet()`: Lancet journal
      – `scale_color_jco()` and `scale_fill_jco()`: Journal of Clinical Oncology

- **Wes Anderson color palettes in the wesanderson R package**. Contains 16 color palettes from Wes Anderson movies.

For example:

```
# jco color palette from the ggsci package
bp + ggsci::scale_fill_jco()
```

```
# Discrete color from wesanderson package
library(wesanderson)
bp + scale_fill_manual(
  values = wes_palette("GrandBudapest1", n = 3)
  )
```

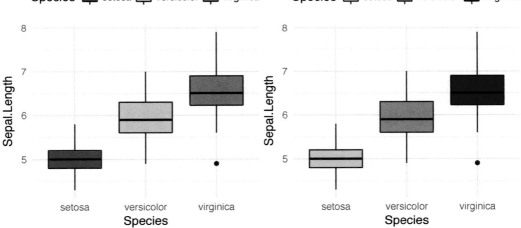

You can find more examples at ggsci package vignettes[1] and at wesanderson github page[2]

7. **Set gradient colors**. For gradient colors, you shoud map the map the argument `color` and/or `fill` to a continuous variable. In the following example, we color points according to the variable: `Sepal.Length`.

```
ggplot(iris, aes(Sepal.Length, Sepal.Width))+
  geom_point(aes(color = Sepal.Length)) +
  scale_color_gradientn(colours = c("blue", "yellow", "red"))+
  theme(legend.position = "right")
```

---

[1] https://cran.r-project.org/web/packages/ggsci/vignettes/ggsci.html
[2] https://github.com/karthik/wesanderson

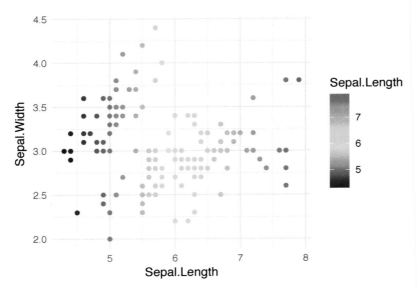

8. **Design and use the power of color palette** at `https://goo.gl/F5g3Lb`

10.9   Points shape, color and size

1. **Common point shapes available in R**:

```
ggpubr::show_point_shapes()+
  theme_void()
```

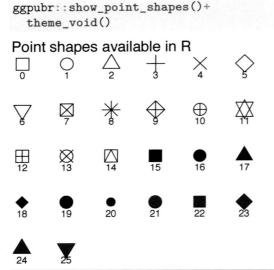

Note that, the point shape options from pch 21 to 25 are open symbols that can be filled by a color. Therefore, you can use the fill argument in geom_point() for these symbols.

2. **Change ggplot point shapes**. The argument `shape` is used, in the function `geom_point()` [ggplot2], for specifying point shapes.

It's also possible to change point shapes and colors by groups. In this case, ggplot2 will use automatically a default color palette and point shapes. You can change manually the appearance of points using the following functions:

- `scale_shape_manual()` : to change manually point shapes
- `scale_color_manual()` : to change manually point colors
- `scale_size_manual()` : to change manually the size of points

Create a scatter plot and change points shape, color and size:

```
# Create a simple scatter plot
ggplot(iris, aes(Sepal.Length, Sepal.Width)) +
  geom_point(shape = 18, color = "#FC4E07", size = 3)+
  theme_minimal()

# Change point shapes and colors by groups
ggplot(iris, aes(Sepal.Length, Sepal.Width)) +
  geom_point(aes(shape = Species, color = Species), size = 3) +
  scale_shape_manual(values = c(5, 16, 17)) +
  scale_color_manual(values = c("#00AFBB", "#E7B800", "#FC4E07"))+
  theme_minimal() +
  theme(legend.position = "top")
```

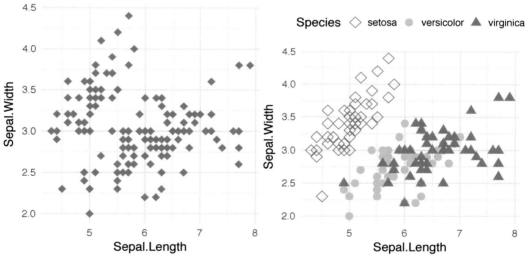

10.10 Line types

1. **Common line types available in R:**

```
ggpubr::show_line_types()+
  theme_gray()
```

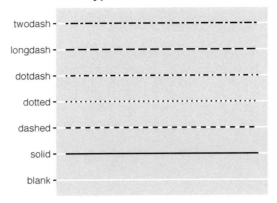

Line types available in R

2. **Change line types.** To change a single line, use for example `linetype = "dashed"`.

In the following R code, we'll change line types and colors by groups. To modify the default colors and line types, the function `scale_color_manual()` and `scale_linetype_manual()` can be used.

```
# Create some data.
# # Compute the mean of `len` grouped by dose and supp
library(dplyr)
df2 <- ToothGrowth %>%
  group_by(dose, supp) %>%
  summarise(len.mean = mean(len))
df2
```

```
## # A tibble: 6 x 3
## # Groups:   dose [?]
##     dose   supp len.mean
##    <fctr> <fctr>    <dbl>
## 1    0.5    OJ    13.23
## 2    0.5    VC     7.98
## 3      1    OJ    22.70
## 4      1    VC    16.77
## 5      2    OJ    26.06
## 6      2    VC    26.14
```

```
# Change manually line type and color manually
ggplot(df2, aes(x = dose, y = len.mean, group = supp)) +
  geom_line(aes(linetype = supp, color = supp))+
  geom_point(aes(color = supp))+
  scale_linetype_manual(values=c("solid", "dashed"))+
  scale_color_manual(values=c("#00AFBB","#FC4E07"))
```

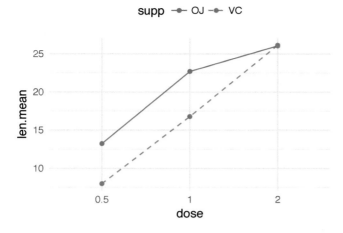

10.11 Rotate a ggplot

Key functions:

- `coord_flip()`: creates horizontal plots
- `scale_x_reverse()` and `scale_y_reverse()`: reverse the axis

```
# Horizontal box plot
ggplot(ToothGrowth, aes(factor(dose), len)) +
  geom_boxplot(fill = "lightgray") +
  theme_bw() +
  coord_flip()

# Reverse y axis
ggplot(mtcars, aes(mpg))+
  geom_density(fill = "lightgray") +
  xlim(0, 40) +
  theme_bw()+
  scale_y_reverse()
```

10.12   Plot annotation

10.12.1   Add straight lines

Key R functions:

- **geom_hline**(yintercept, linetype, color, size): add horizontal lines
- **geom_vline**(xintercept, linetype, color, size): add vertical lines
- **geom_abline**(intercept, slope, linetype, color, size): add regression lines
- **geom_segment**(): add segments

Create a simple scatter plot:

- **Creating a simple scatter plot**

```
sp <- ggplot(data = mtcars, aes(x = wt, y = mpg)) +
  geom_point()+theme_bw()
```

- **Add straight lines and segments**

```
# Add horizontal line at y = 20; and vertical line at x = 3
sp + geom_hline(yintercept = 20, linetype = "dashed", color = "red") +
  geom_vline(xintercept = 3, color = "blue", size = 1)

# Add regression line
sp + geom_abline(intercept = 37, slope = -5, color="blue")+
  labs(title = "y = -5X + 37")

# Add a vertical line segment from
# point A(4, 15) to point B(4, 27)
sp + geom_segment(x = 4, y = 15, xend = 4, yend = 27)
```

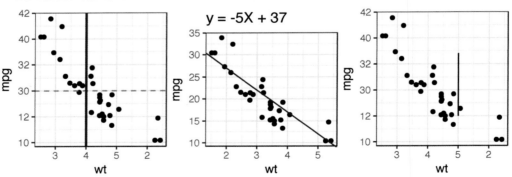

- **Add arrows, curves and rectangles:**

```
# Add arrow at the end of the segment
require(grid)
sp + geom_segment(x = 5, y = 30, xend = 3.5, yend = 25,
                  arrow = arrow(length = unit(0.5, "cm")))

# Add curves
```

```
sp + geom_curve(aes(x = 2, y = 15, xend = 3, yend = 15))

# Add rectangles
ggplot(data = mtcars, aes(x = wt, y = mpg)) +
  geom_rect(xmin = 3, ymin = -Inf, xmax = 4, ymax = Inf,
            fill = "lightgray") +
  geom_point() + theme_bw()
```

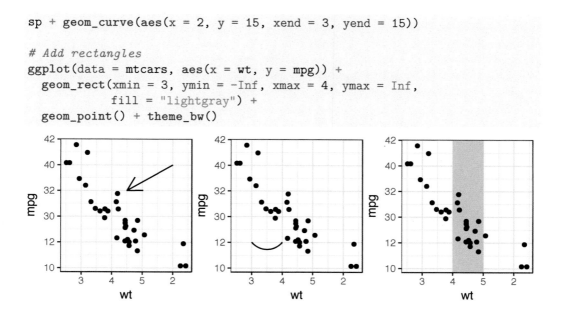

10.12.2 Text annotation

Key ggplot2 function:

- **geom_text**(): adds text directly to the plot
- **geom_label**(): draws a rectangle underneath the text, making it easier to read.
- **annotate**(): useful for adding small text annotations at a particular location on the plot
- **annotation_custom**(): Adds static annotations that are the same in every panel

```
# Add text at a particular coordinate
sp + annotate("text", x = 3, y = 30,
              label = "Scatter plot",
              color = "red", fontface = 2)
```

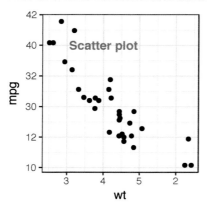

Bibliography

Aphalo, P. J. (2017). *ggpmisc: Miscellaneous Extensions to 'ggplot2'*. R package version 0.2.15.

Attali, D. (2017). *ggExtra: Add Marginal Histograms to 'ggplot2', and More 'ggplot2' Enhancements*. R package version 0.7.1.

Horikoshi, M. and Tang, Y. (2017). *ggfortify: Data Visualization Tools for Statistical Analysis Results*. R package version 0.4.1.

Kassambara, A. (2016). *ggcorrplot: Visualization of a Correlation Matrix using 'ggplot2'*. R package version 0.1.1.9000.

Kassambara, A. (2017). *ggpubr: 'ggplot2' Based Publication Ready Plots*. R package version 0.1.5.999.

Kassambara, A. and Mundt, F. (2017). *factoextra: Extract and Visualize the Results of Multivariate Data Analyses*. R package version 1.0.5.999.

Ligges, U., Maechler, M., and Schnackenberg, S. (2017). *scatterplot3d: 3D Scatter Plot*. R package version 0.3-40.

Pedersen, T. L. (2016). *ggforce: Accelerating 'ggplot2'*. R package version 0.1.1.

Sarkar, D. (2016). *lattice: Trellis Graphics for R*. R package version 0.20-34.

Schloerke, B., Crowley, J., Cook, D., Briatte, F., Marbach, M., Thoen, E., Elberg, A., and Larmarange, J. (2016). *GGally: Extension to 'ggplot2'*. R package version 1.3.0.

Sidiropoulos, N., Sohi, S. H., Rapin, N., and Bagger, F. O. (2015). Sinaplot: an enhanced chart for simple and truthful representation of single observations over multiple classes. *bioRxiv*.

Wickham, H. and Chang, W. (2017). *ggplot2: Create Elegant Data Visualisations Using the Grammar of Graphics*. http://ggplot2.tidyverse.org, https://github.com/tidyverse/ggplot2.

Wickham, H., Francois, R., Henry, L., and Müller, K. (2017). *dplyr: A Grammar of Data Manipulation*. R package version 0.7.4.

Wilke, C. O. (2017). *ggridges: Ridgeline Plots in 'ggplot2'*. R package version 0.4.1.

Index

Made in the USA
Middletown, DE
10 August 2019